MINISTERS

of

FIRST

CHRISTIAN CHURCH

(Disciples of Christ)

SPRINGFIELD, ILLINOIS

1833 — 1962

MINISTERS
of
FIRST CHRISTIAN CHURCH
(Disciples of Christ)

SPRINGFIELD, ILLINOIS
1833 - 1962

by

CHARLES FOSTER McELROY

Printed
as a private edition by

THE BETHANY PRESS

Manufactured in the United States of America

$5.00

To the memory of
my companion and comrade
Cora Clarke McElroy

FOREWORD

Church historian and elder emeritus, Charles Foster McElroy, now in his eighty-sixth year, goes to his office every day as attorney-consultant-adviser for the Department of Revenue, State of Illinois. He has devoted much of the rest of his time for nearly four years to the necessary research, correspondence, and writing involved in the publication of this book of historical and contemporary interest.

When Dr. William F. Rothenburger was pastor of the Springfield First Christian Church from 1917-27, he compiled biographical sketches of eleven former pastors and assembled other data in a scrapbook with this handwritten introduction:

> In order that the rich history of First Christian Church throughout ninety-four years might be preserved to future generations, all available historical sketches have been compiled and bound into this volume. While they are necessarily fragmentary, they will nevertheless provide succeeding generations with a knowledge of the trend of events throughout almost a century (save six years) of rich history. Compiler, Wm. F. Rothenburger, June, 1927.

Another stimulus to Mr. McElroy was the suggestion by one of his later pastors, Harry M. Davis (1951-1955) that portraits of former ministers be procured. Mr. McElroy has followed through on this suggestion, adding portraits not only of ministers, but of their wives, and also of living link missionaries. With the artistry of photographer Herbert Georg, who is able to produce a beautiful portrait from an old or damaged snapshot or newspaper picture, Mr. McElroy has assembled a collection of fifty-one portraits of twenty-four pastors, twenty-one wives, and six missionaries. These portraits were presented to the church by Mr. McElroy as a memorial to his wife, Cora Clarke McElroy. Their son and his wife, Mr. and Mrs. George Clarke McElroy of Chicago, were present when this unique and valued collection was dedicated in special services on September 21, 1958. The Disciples of Christ Historical Society, Nashville, Tennessee, felt that this collection of portraits, which is displayed in the spacious hall east of the sanctuary, should be augmented by a compilation of biographical information regarding these church leaders. In three years' time Mr. McElroy's research has taken him to college and library centers in many sections of the country, and he has been in correspondence with relatives and interested church people from coast to coast.

With perfectly amazing persistence of vision, sense of mission, and tenacity of purpose, Mr. McElroy has brought this work to its present state of readiness for publication. It is particularly appropriate that those who find an interest in this volume should come also to know more about the author.

Charles Foster McElroy, son of George Washington McElroy and Laura Foster McElroy, was born April 26, 1876, on a farm in Red Willow County, Nebraska. His father, a graduate of the Eureka College Bible Department in 1874, served as state evangelist in central Illinois for two years. He held a revival meeting in a schoolhouse at a country crossroads called Blooming Grove, about 35 miles southwest of Springfield, between Palmyra and Girard, with 48 additions, resulting in the formation of a congregation. He became the first pastor, and in 1874 caused the erection of a frame church building which is still in use. One of the charter members was Miss Laura Ophelia Foster, daughter of Dr. Robert Foster, physician and pioneer preacher. She and George W. McElroy were married April 25, 1875. They then took up a homestead in southwestern Nebraska. Due to a devastating raid by grasshoppers, and fears of an attack by the Indians, they moved to Kansas. After the father died in 1880 the family returned to Illinois. Charles was about three and a half years older than his boyhood friend, Vachel Lindsay.

Mr. McElroy attended Eureka College for two years, where he played on the first basketball team. He is a graduate of Butler University, 1904, and received his law degree, J.D., from the University of Chicago in 1915. He has traveled to all continents and visited thirty-eight foreign countries. He can be found in the cast of a play at the Springfield Theatre Guild or on a special bus loaded with young people en route to a Springfield High School basketball game. Although not the oldest member in age, he holds the longest membership in First Christian Church, having been baptized by Elder John B. Briney in November, 1890. He served two terms as chairman of the General Board of the church. During the last three years (1959-1961) he has been a member of the Committee on Recommendations of the International Convention of Christian Churches (Disciples of Christ). He is a life member of the Art Institute of Chicago and of the Disciples of Christ Historical Society and is a director of the Vachel Lindsay House Fund, Inc., which purchased and restored the Lindsay home and made it a shrine for visitors.

He toured Mexico in 1954; visited Latin-American mission stations in South America in 1956; went around the world in 1958; went on an extended bus tour of "Landmarks of Disciple History" in 1959; attended the World Convention of Christian Churches (Disciples of Christ) in Edinburgh, Scotland, and toured Scandinavia in 1960.

In the summer of 1961 he was hailed as a world champion at the American Shakespeare Festival Theatre and Academy in Stratford, Connecticut. He had just cōme from the Bard's Playhouse in Stratford, Ontario, where he had seen Shakespeare's play, *Coriolanus.* While in Connecticut he saw *Troilus and Cressida* starring Jessica Tandy. One of the proudest boasts of the late George Bernard Shaw was that he had seen 27 different plays of Shakespeare, more than anyone else in the world. Charles F. McElroy produced an authenticated list of the 30 which he has seen, beginning with *Antony and Cleopatra* which he saw in Springfield in 1899. The press representatives of the American Shakespeare Festival thought that this was significant enough to warrant publicity. They arranged for Mr. McElroy to present a rare Shakespearean mug to that theater's growing collection, and to have it accepted by Jessica Tandy, the leading star of the 1961 season's company. She appeared as "Lady Macbeth," and as "Cassandra" in *Troilus and Cressida.*

No one else could have, or would have, written this book. We are all indebted to Mr. McElroy for the compilation and preservation of these historical materials.

—Beryl Sales Kinser, minister,
First Christian Church
Springfield, Illinois

ACKNOWLEDGMENTS

1. The longest and most authoritative history of First Christian Church was prepared by Charles P. Kane, a long-time elder of the church, who was county judge of Sangamon County, 1892-1896. It is entitled

The Christian Church of Springfield, Illinois
Something of Its Beginning and Growth,
During the First Sixty Years of Its History.
1833-1893

It appears on pages 298-314 of *Transactions of the Illinois State Historical Society for the Year 1907.* On page 314 is the following:

> (Note: The foregoing paper was read at the celebration, by the Christian Church of Springfield, Illinois, at the Sixtieth Anniversary of its organization, observed the first Sunday in October, A.D. 1893).

This history has been printed separately and copies are in the Illinois State Historical Library.

2. Mrs. Mary Logan Coleman Morrison (Mrs. Hugh T. Morrison) prepared *Historical Sketch of the First Christian Church on the Occasion of the Seventy-fifth Anniversary, 1908.* A typewritten copy is in a book among the prized historical material of our church.

3. Her husband, Dr. Hugh T. Morrison, prepared a *History of First Christian Church, Springfield, Illinois,* which he read

at the laying of the cornerstone of the present building on August 1, 1911.

4. B. R. Hieronymus, a long-time elder, wrote *Historical Sketch of the First Christian Church* which was read at the West Side Christian Church at an afternoon memorial on December 6, 1914.

5. B. R. Hieronymus also prepared *Recollections of Fifty Years* for the annual church meeting of January, 1922, but because of his illness it was read by Mrs. Vachel T. Lindsay.

6. Mrs. Mary L. Morrison also wrote *Historical Review, October, 1923, . . . on occasion of the Celebration of the Ninetieth Anniversary, 1833-1923.* A copy is in the Illinois State Historical Library.

7. In the memorial booklet issued on the occasion of the Centennial Celebration in 1933, there appears a historical sketch in the nature of short items telling of significant events in the progress of the congregation. The author or compiler is not known.

8. At the 125th anniversary on April 23, 1958, a memorial volume, prepared by Chester E. Hahn and Beulah Gordon in a narrative form, was issued.

The author has drawn freely on these histories.

The source of much of the information about Alexander Graham is Lawson, P. B., *The Life and Character, To Which are Added Some of the Addresses and Sermons of Alexander Graham, Teacher of the Christian Church in Marion, Alabama.* New York: John F. Trow, Printer, 49 Ann-Street, 1853. This is bound in *The Gospel Advocate,* Volume II, 1856, Disciples of Christ Historical Society, Nashville, Tennessee.

At this point, I wish to make special mention of the services of my predecessor as church historian, Albert W. Hillier, for his painstaking care in preserving and organizing data of all kinds which make up what may be called the archives of the church.

In compiling this book, my aim has been to take advantage of whatever is already in print, including biographies, magazine articles, newspaper clippings, obituaries, and other printed matter, as being most authoritative, in order to obtain so far as possible a contemporary record and appraisal. This necessarily has required the cooperation of many individuals and institutions, to whom thanks are due.

The source of the largest amount of material has been the Illinois State Historical Library, of which Miss Mary Moyer is head cataloguer; next the records and library of the United Christian Missionary Society, Indianapolis, Indiana, of which Doris Autrey is director. Next is the library of the Disciples of Christ Historical Society at Nashville, Tennessee, of which Dr. Claude E. Spencer is the curator. Use of the library facilities and the assistance of the staff have been made available also by the following institutions:

Bethany College, Bethany, West Virginia; Robert H. Yockey, librarian.

Christian Theological Seminary, Butler University, Indianapolis, Indiana; Henry K. Shaw, librarian.

Disciples Divinity House of the University of Chicago, Chicago, Illinois; Jay R. Calhoun, assistant dean.

Eureka College, Eureka, Illinois; Norma C. Brown, chairman, Division of Off-campus Information and Service.

Hiram College, Hiram, Ohio; Lawrence C. Underwood, registrar.

Transylvania College, Lexington, Kentucky; Pearl Anderson, registrar.

I express particular thanks and appreciation to the persons who have contributed complete biographies of some pastors, including:

W. E. Garrison for Charles Clayton Morrison; Beulah Gordon for F. W. Burnham; Ronald E. Osborn for E. V. Zollars; Woodrow W. Wasson for Alexander Graham; Edmund

Wilkes, Jr., for S. E. Pearre and L. B. Wilkes.

For providing portions of certain biographies, I extend thanks to the following:

Richard Dickinson, Eureka, Illinois, for D. R. Howe; Mrs. Campbellina D. (Mrs. Herbert G.) Odell, La Jolla, California, for T. T. Holton; Dr. Homer Wilson Carpenter, Louisville, Kentucky, for J. B. Briney; Mrs. Grace Everest McDade, McDade Lane, Chattanooga, Tennessee, for H. W. Everest; J. Edward Moseley, Indianapolis, Indiana, for W. F. Rothenburger.

Chas. C. Ware, curator of the Carolina Discipliana Library, Wilson, North Carolina, has furnished material for a considerable number of these biographies.

Locally, my chief co-worker has been Mary Moyer, who officially is assistant church historian, and who is head cataloguer of the Illinois State Historical Library. She has made available the resources of that and other libraries, and has assisted in revision.

Of special importance has been the sympathetic co-operation and guidance of our pastor and wife, Dr. and Mrs. Beryl S. Kinser. Dr. Kinser has shared with me the facilities of his office at the church, and has collaborated in writing numerous letters in the search for data, as well as writing the Foreword for this volume. My thanks to the pastor's secretary, Mrs. John Nolan, and to Jane Ann Kinser for stenographic services.

Naturally, I cannot name all who deserve mention for their helpfulness. I extend thanks for the assistance of numerous members of the church and others, in typing and research.

CHARLES FOSTER MCELROY

OUR CHURCH BUILDINGS

The congregation of First Christian Church, Springfield, Illinois, was organized April 23, 1833. At first it met in homes of members, mostly in the homes of Philo Beers and Stephen T. Logan; also in the "carding machine" at the northwest corner of Fourth Street and Capitol Avenue, and also in the courthouse. The carding machine, which appears to have been used generally for public gatherings, never belonged to the congregation and is not considered one of its church buildings.

In the Illinois State Historical Library is a "Historical Review" written by Mrs. Mary Coleman Morrison on the occasion of the celebration of the ninetieth anniversary of the church, 1833-1923. In it she refers to the structures that have housed this congregation as follows:

The first church building was erected within the first year, in 1834, on a fifty-foot lot on the north side of Madison between Fourth and Fifth Streets where the A. L. Ide & Sons Foundry is now located. The lot cost Sixty Dollars. In order to erect a building (40′ x 60′) funds had to be solicited from those outside the membership of the church. There would be many times when this struggling congregation would not be using the building, so the condition on which sufficient funds were forthcoming was that the building be also available for other groups at convenient times. This condition was lived up to, but it led to trouble when the Mormons came in 1839. After one or two of the members had been "captured" by them, a petition was circulated, securing the consent of the contributors to the withdrawal of

First building, dedicated 1834

this condition. This was granted. The Mormons no longer used the building and thus the building became the property of the Christian Church.

The record of February 15, 1852, shows that a committee consisting of Jonathan R. Saunders, Stephen T. Logan (Lincoln's second law partner), William F. Elkin, William Lavely, and Joseph W. Bennett was appointed to make arrangements for a "more suitable house of worship." The old building was sold to the Free Portuguese Congregation. A new lot at the northeast corner of Sixth and Jefferson Streets was purchased at a cost of $1,300.00 and a building 40′ by 60′ erected under the contractorship of Joseph W. Bennett. This second building was dedicated in 1853.

In 1880 a building committee composed of L. H. Coleman, Aaron Thompson, H. C. Latham, Erwin Clark, W. D. Logan, A. H. Saunders, and Mrs. Hathaway Pasfield was appointed. The lot on the northwest corner of Fifth and Jackson Streets was purchased for $2,200.00, and the building erected thereon was dedicated February 12, 1882. The last meeting in this third building was held on June 26, 1910. The congregation met in the Masonic Temple until the present building was ready for occupancy.

As early as 1908 there was definite consideration of a new building, but the formal action came early in 1909. Frederick

Second building, dedicated 1853

W. Burnham, pastor, was appointed chairman of the building committee whose other members were Hathaway Pasfield, Mary L. Morrison, Charles P. Kane, and Grandville A. Hulett. The lot and building at Fifth and Jackson Streets were sold for $34,000.00, and the present lot at the southeast corner of Sixth and Cook Streets was purchased from E. A. Hall for $17,000.00. The address given by Mrs. Caroline Beers Kane when she turned the first spade of ground preparatory to the

Third building, dedicated 1882

erection of this building is recorded in the minutes of June 4, 1911. Caroline, at the age of 6, had attended the organization meeting in the carding machine, hence had a personal connection of 78 years with all these buildings.

The service of laying the cornerstone was held at three o'clock on the afternoon of August 1, 1911. Elwood Commandery No. 6 of Knights Templar acted as escort for the Grand Lodge of Illinois, A. F. & A. M. The program included a historical statement read by Dr. H. T. Morrison and address by Reverend Finis S. Idleman, pastor of Central Church of Christ of Des Moines, Iowa. The cornerstone was laid with Masonic ceremonies by A. B. Ashley, Grand Master of the Grand Lodge of Illinois. The building was dedicated June 23, 1912. F. M. Rains, president of the American Christian Missionary Society, delivered the dedicatory sermon.

The *World Call* of August, 1921, contains a feature article on "Church Architecture" by Sherman Kirk. It carries a one-half-page picture of our church building, and says: "Perhaps the finest example of Gothic style in which a congregation of the Disciples of Christ worship is the splendid building of the First Church in Springfield, Illinois."

Statement of Cost of New Building (Submitted by Trustees Jan. 1, 1913).

McKee Construction Co.	$ 81,429.18
Austin Organ Co.	5,412.22
Patterson Stewart—heat-ventilating	4,801.80
Von Gerichten Art Glass	4,550.72
R. Haas Electric Mfg. Co.	4,374.65
Vaught Furniture Co.	4,010.00
S. R. Badgley	3,029.04
Jackson Electric	1,544.66
Johnston & Hatcher furniture & rugs	1,191.53

W. B. Miller & Son	1,050.40
S. A. Bullard, architect	800.00
G. H. Schanbacher, decorating	700.00
Wallis curbing and sodding	556.88
Spencer Vacuum Turbine	500.00
Kitchen equipment	420.35
Paullin-Patterson—painting	250.00
Bible school cabinets and furniture	151.51
John Bressmer—furnishing and rugs	146.00
French & Company—piano	120.00
	$115,038.94

Incidental expenses incurred during building period:

E. A. Hall, interest on mortgage notes	$1,875.00
Masonic Temple	1,350.00
Interest on note to bank	1,270.76
Miscellaneous incidentals	608.72
Insurance on building, organ, and furniture 5 yrs.	592.50
Jefferson Company—printing	184.30
	$5,881.28
Credit by interest received from sale of old church	$1,865.61
	$4,015.67

The Influence of Melrose Abbey

It is a commonly accepted fact that Dr. Burnham came to this congregation primarily to give the church the benefit of his experience as a church builder. He had just completed and dedicated a new church building at Decatur for the Central Church of Christ. Our congregation had in view a new structure to replace the one at Fifth and Jackson Streets. Dr. and Mrs. Burnham spent several months on a European tour, forming impressions and gathering ideas. Among other places, they visited the ruins of Melrose Abbey, about forty miles from Edinburgh, Scotland. They considered the kirk of the Abbey as the one structure whose main features were most adaptable to the building at Springfield. They obtained sketches and plans, and on their return recommended that these be used in so far as practicable. The building committee agreed. In Mrs. Mary L. Morrison's "Historical Review" for the ninetieth anniversary, 1833-1923, she says: "It was suggested to the architect, Sidney R. Badgley, of Cleveland, that he use all the architectural effects of Melrose Abbey that could be fitted into a church which would meet the needs of the twentieth century."

Ruins of Melrose Abbey

The kirk (church) in Melrose Abbey was completed in 1146, as part of a large group of buildings built by the Cistercian Order of Monks, in the valley of the Tweed River, about 40 miles northwest of Edinburgh, in Roxburghshire, Scotland. During the religious wars of the middle ages, it was repeatedly pillaged and destroyed. Practically all of the buildings are entirely gone except the kirk, a considerable portion

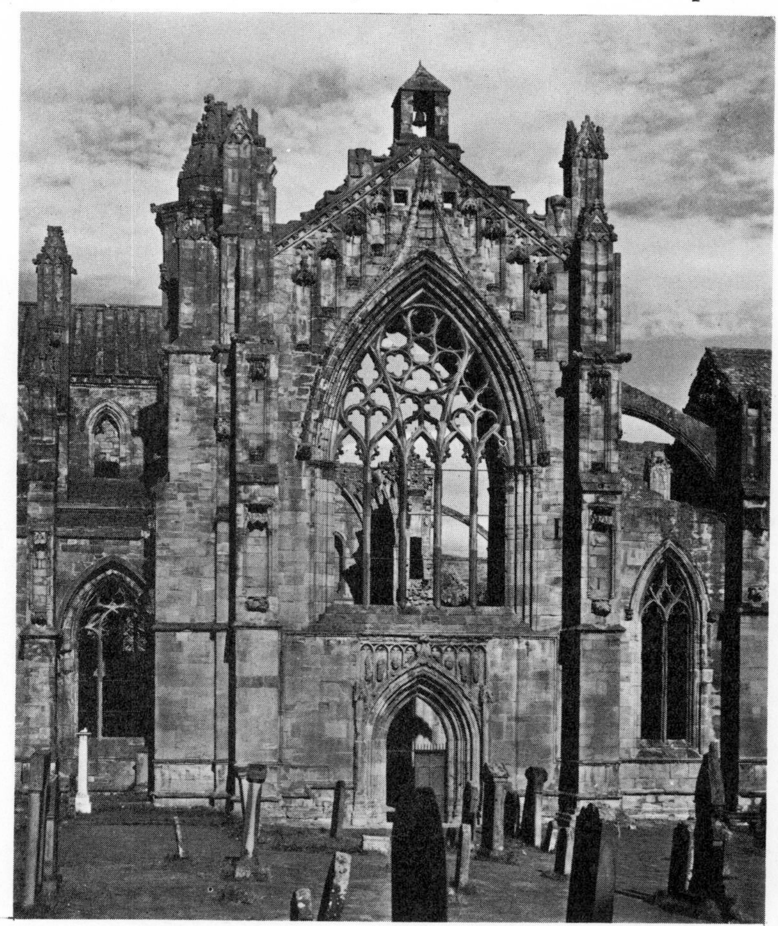

Ruins of Melrose Abbey

of which is still standing. For several hundred years it has been in ruins, but what is left is well cared for and continues to be a shrine for tourists and visitors.

In the summer of 1960, Dr. and Mrs. Kinser and Charles Foster McElroy, while attending the World Convention of Disciples of Christ at Edinburgh, Scotland, made a side trip to the ruins of Melrose Abbey. They noted the similarity of the kirk to our church in general appearance, both outside and inside, and in the proportions of nave, transept, and apse.

The caretaker displayed pictures of noted buildings which have adapted features from Melrose Abbey, but he had no picture of the Springfield church. On his return the church historian sent several pictures of the church building, and the caretaker wrote as follows:

Mr. C. McElroy
c/o First Christian Church

Melrose Abbey
Melrose
Roxburghshire
Scotland
Sept. 20th
1960

Dear Sir,

On behalf of myself & my colleagues I wish to thank you for your kindness in sending the post cards of your church. We were all quite impressed by its outward appearance. I can well imagine the beauty of its interior. I hope you had an enjoyable holiday in our country & could see most of the things it had to offer, in spite of the inclement weather. Once again we say thank you.

Yours truly,
A. Jackson.
H/Custodian

On May 1, 1926, crosses brought from Solomon's quarry by Dr. Burnham, and from Gethsemane by the pastor, Dr. William F. Rothenburger, were placed in the chancel and dedicated.

In 1932 the pastor, Clark Walker Cummings, placed in the chancel floor stones from Calvary and a Crusader tile from Seville, Spain.

In the rear wall of the sanctuary is a block of travertine stone from the Roman Colosseum, and on the west wall of the narthex is a stone from the foundation of the Brush Run Church, Kentucky, the first church building erected by Disciples of Christ.

On the north side of the narthex is a dark stone brought by Dr. Rothenburger from Ahorey, Ireland, where Thomas Campbell preached from 1798 to 1807.

In 1914 the education building was remodeled, and what had been an auditorium was converted into classrooms on first and second floors.

In 1918 the Dengen chimes were presented by Mrs. Mary C. Freeman in memory of her husband, C. W. Freeman, at a cost of $7,000.00. They were replaced in 1923.

ROSTER OF PASTORS

1.	Josephus Hewitt (Hewett)	1833-1835
2.	Alexander Graham	1837-1838
3.	Jeremiah P. Lancaster	1841-1843
4.	William M. Brown	1843-1847
5.	Andrew Jackson Kane	1847-1851
6.	John H. Hughes	1851-1852
7.	Alexander Johnson (Johnston)	1852-1854
8.	B. F. Perky	1854-1856
9.	Sterling Elwood Pearre	1856-1862
10.	Daniel Radcliffe Howe	1862-1864
11.	Lanceford Bramblett Wilkes	1866-1868
12.	Thomas Tilgham Holton	1868-1870
13.	James B. Crane (Crain)	1871-1872
14.	Harvey William Everest	1873-1874
15.	Edward Thomas Williams	1875-1877
16.	John Milton Atwater	1878-1879
17.	Joseph Buford Allen	1879-1883
18.	John Z. Taylor	1883-1884
19.	Ely Vaughn Zollars	1885-1888
20.	John Benton Briney	1888-1891
21.	Abner Peter Cobb	1891-1897
22.	Jay Elwood Lynn	1898-1902

23.	Hugh Tucker Morrison, Jr., copastor	1902-1904
24.	Charles Clayton Morrison, copastor	1902-1904
	pastor	1905-1906
25.	Frederick William Burnham	1907-1914
26.	Frank Waller Allen	1914-1917
27.	William Frederic Rothenburger	1918-1927
28.	Clark Walker Cummings	1928-1937
29.	Charles Benson Tupper	1937-1951
30.	Harry McCuan Davis	1951-1955
31.	James Nicholas Gibble (ad interim)	1955-1957
32.	Beryl Sales Kinser	1957-

Josephus Hewitt

Pastor 1833-1835

BORN: August 27, 1805, at New York City
DIED: About 1868, at Natchez, Mississippi
MARRIED: Lucilla H. Payne

It was the preaching of Josephus Hewitt (sometimes spelled Hewett) that led to the organization of the original Christian Church in Springfield. Mr. Hewitt came to Illinois about 1830, and lived near Jacksonville. As a preacher he assisted Barton W. Stone in several evangelistic meetings and was a charter member of the Jacksonville Christian Church, which was organized by Stone. He was urged by various persons to come to Springfield to organize a church. He first preached at a carding machine building, but his audiences were so large that services had to be held in the courthouse. In the *Sangamo Journal* of March 16, 1833, is the announcement: "Rev. Josephus Hewitt of Jacksonville will preach in the Court House, in this town today and tomorrow—services to commence at 11 A.M." In the same paper, on November 16, 1933: "We are requested to say that Mr. Hewitt is expected to preach at the Court House today at 11 o'clock, and on Sunday."

Judge Charles P. Kane, in his history of First Christian Church, says that Hewitt was the "first minister of the gospel to promulgate at Springfield that interpretation of Biblical teaching, accepted and advocated by the body of believers known as the Christian Church or the Disciples of Christ."[1] His converts were baptized in the Sangamon River. Many placed their memberships in various existing churches, but one group met at the home of Mrs. Garner Goodan and organized a congregation consisting of the following twelve charter members:

Philo and Martha Beers	Mrs. Ann McNabb
Joseph and Lucy Bennett	Reuben Radford
Alfred and Martha Elder	William Shoup

[1]*The Christian Church of Springfield, Illinois, Something of its Beginning and Growth, During the First Sixty Years of its History, 1833-1893.* Charles P. Kane, reprinted from the Transactions of the Illinois State Historical Society, 1907, page 5.

Mrs. Garner Goodan — Elisha Tabor
Dr. James R. Gray

To these were soon added:

America T. Logan (wife of Stephen T. Logan, Lincoln's second law partner)
General James Adams — Mordecai Mobley and wife
Col. E. D. Baker and wife — Woodworth family
George Bennett and wife — and others
Lemuel and Evaline Higby

Judge Kane also states in his history:

> Mr. Hewitt was a remarkable man. He had qualities that would have distinguished him in any society, in any age. Large of stature, dignified of mien, he at once impressed individual or assemblage. As a speaker he was effective and forcible.
>
> Mr. Hewitt became one of the most noted lawyers of that day, and is spoken of by the older members of the profession as a man of strong mind and very eloquent in his pleadings.[2]
>
> He was admitted to the bar, and was appointed prosecuting attorney for this district. He was a conscientious man and had a high sense of the responsibilities of his office. On the first day of each term of court, it was his duty to charge the Grand Jury, and people invariably laid aside their work and flocked to the court room to hear him. While in the height of his power and usefulness an event occurred which changed his whole career and took him from among us. [The event was an argument between Hewitt, Lincoln, Baker and Logan with respect to a murder trial.] . . . I never saw Josephus Hewitt again. The next morning it was announced that he had resigned his office and gone south, and one of the most eloquent men Springfield ever knew faded from the recollection of its inhabitants.[3]

Upon leaving Springfield in 1838, Hewitt moved to Natchez, Mississippi. There is no record that he practiced law there, but he became active in Whig politics. The date of his death is believed to be about 1868.

---

[2] *The Bench and Bar of Illinois*, edited by John M. Palmer, Chicago, The Lewis Publishing Company, 1899. Volume 1, pages 173-174.

[3] *Some Forgotten Orators: Recollections of Judge J. H. Matheny*, in *Illinois State Journal* of April 28, 1889.

Edgar DeWitt Jones, in his book *Lincoln and the Preachers,* says:

During Mr. Lincoln's Springfield years some of his closest ministerial friendships were made. Such a one was the Rev. Josephus Hewett who organized the First Christian Church (Disciples) in that city. He was an evangelist of that communion known popularly in those days by the nickname "Campbellites," due to the fact that one of the founders of the movement was Alexander Campbell of Bethany, West Virginia. That the Rev. Mr. Hewett was a warm friend of Lincoln is evidenced by the letter Mr. Lincoln wrote from Congress in 1848. Lincoln addressed him as "Dear Hewett" . . .[4]

The letter from Lincoln to Hewett follows:

Washington, Feb. 13, 1848.

Dear Hewett:

Your whig representative from Mississippi, P. W. Tompkins[5] has just shown me a letter of yours to him. I am jealous because you did not write to me—Perhaps you have forgotten me—Don't you remember a long black fellow who rode on horseback with you from Tremont to Springfield nearly ten years ago, swiming your horses over the Mackinaw on the trip? Well, I am that same one fellow yet—I was once of your opinion, expressed in your letter, that presidential electors should be dispensed with; but a more thorough knowledge of the causes that first introduced them, has made me doubt—Those causes were briefly these—The convention that framed the constitution had this difficulty: the small states wished to so frame the new government as that they might be equal to the large ones regardless of the inequality of population; the large ones insisted on equality in proportion to population. They compromised it, by basing the House of Representatives on *population,* and the Senate on *states* regardless of population; and the executive on both principles, by electors in each state, equal in numbers to her senators *and* representatives. Now, throw away the machinery of electors, and the compromise is broken up, and the whole yielded to the principle of the large states—There is one thing more—in the slave states, you have representatives, and consequently, electors, partly

---

[4]*Lincoln and the Preachers* by Edgar DeWitt Jones, (New York: Harper & Brothers, 1948), page 21.

[5]Patrick W. Tompkins was a Whig who stayed at the same boarding house in Washington, D. C., as Lincoln did.

upon the basis of your black population, which would be swept away by the change you seem to think desirable. Have you ever reflected on these things?

But to come to the main point, I wish you to know that I have made a speech in congress, and that I want you to be *enlightened* by reading it; to further which object, I send a copy of the speech by this mail.

For old acquaintance sake, if for nothing else, be sure to write me on receiving this. I was very near forgetting to tell you that on my being introduced to Genl. Quitman,[6] and telling him I was from Springfield, Illinois, he at once remarked "Then you are acquainted with my valued friend Hewett of Natchez," and on being assured I was, he said just such things about you as I like to hear said about my own valued friends. Yours as ever.

A. Lincoln

[6]John A. Quitman, Democrat and lawyer, was a major-general in the regular army in 1847.

A copy of this letter in Lincoln's handwriting, made from a photostat in the Library of Congress, is reproduced here, by courtesy of the Illinois State Historical Library.

Washington Feb. 13. 1848-

Dear Hewett:

Your whig representative from Mississippi P. W. Tompkins, has just shown me a letter of yours to him- I am jealous because you did not write to me- Perhaps you have forgotten me- Dont you remember a long black fellow who rode on horseback with you from Tremont to Springfield nearly ten years ago, swimming your horses over the Mackinaw on the trip? Well, I am that same one fellow yet- I was once of your opinion, expressed in your letter, that presidential electors should be dispensed with; but a more thorough knowledge of the causes that first introduced them, has made me doubt- Those causes were briefly these- The convention that framed the constitution had this difficulty: the small states wished to so frame the new government as that they might be equal to the large ones regardless of the inequality of population; the large ones insisted on equality in proportion to population- They compromised it, by basing the House of Representatives on population, and the Senate on states regardless of population; and the executive on both principles, by electors in each state, equal in number to her senators and representatives— Now, throw away the machinery of electors, and the compromise is broken up, and the whole yielded to the principle of the large states— There is one thing more— In the slave states, you have representatives, and consequently, electors, partly upon the basis of your black population, which would be swept away by the change you seem to think desireable— Have you ever reflected on these things?

But to come to the main point, I wish you to know that I have made a speech in congress, and that I want you to be enlightened by reading it; to further which object, I send you a copy of the speech by this mail—

For old acquaintance sake, if for nothing else, be sure to write me on receiving this— I was very near forgetting to tell you that on my being introduced to Genl. Quitman, and telling him I was from Springfield, Illinois, he at once remarked "Then you are acquainted with my valued friend Hewett of Natchez", and on being assured I was, he said just such things about you as I like to hear said about my own valued friends—

Yours as ever
A. Lincoln

Lincoln's friendship with Josephus Hewitt was not his only connection with the congregation of this church. In 1842 Lincoln was defeated in the primary for the nomination as a Whig candidate for Congress by Edward D. Baker, who with his wife had become members of this church during the pastorate of Josephus Hewitt. Baker was elected and served one term in Congress, and was succeeded by Lincoln in 1844.

The rapid growth of the Disciples in central Illinois is curiously confirmed by the testimony of Lincoln's biographers. In 1842 Lincoln, as a candidate for Congress, sought the support of the Whigs of Sangamon County (in which Springfield is located) in a primary election, but was defeated by Edward Baker, "a Disciple preacher." Nicolay and Hay, Barton, and Beveridge agree that Baker's success was largely due to the backing he received from the Disciples. Albert J. Beveridge's *Abraham Lincoln* says: "Baker had all the 'Campbellites,' to whose church he belonged." W. E. Barton's *Life of Abraham Lincoln* quotes Lincoln as saying: "Baker is a Campbellite; and therefore, as I suppose, with few exceptions, got that church" (Volume 1, p. 275). Nicolay and Hay's *Abraham Lincoln, A History,* as published serially, is even more specific:

> Baker and his wife belonged to that numerous and powerful sect which has several times played so important a part in Western politics—the Disciples. They all supported him energetically, and used as arguments against Lincoln that his wife was a Presbyterian, that most of her family were Episcopalians, that Lincoln himself belonged to no church and that he was suspected of deism, and, finally, that he was the candidate of the aristocracy. (*Century Magazine,* Nov., 1886, p. 392.)

Baker was English by birth, a lawyer by profession, a Disciple chiefly by marriage, and a preacher only occasionally. He was a brilliant speaker, a firm friend of Lincoln, who named a son after him, and later a United States senator from Oregon and a colonel in the Union Army until he was killed in the battle of Ball's Bluff. That the Disciples were powerful enough in Sangamon County to determine the outcome of an election in 1842 seems improbable. The *Berean,* a small magazine edited by A. Graham and published for one year, reports (Jan., 1838) that the Springfield church at that time had ninety members and adds that Schuyler, the second county west of Sangamon, had four churches and about 150 members, including "many dispersed Disciples."[7]

What may be termed a third tie-in of Lincoln with this congregation is the fact that his second law partner was Judge Stephen T. Logan, whose wife, America T. Logan, became a member in 1833, soon after the congregation was organized.

[7]The incident is related in *The Disciples of Christ,* Winfred E. Garrison and Alfred T. De Groot (St. Louis: Bethany Press, 1948), pp. 221-222.

Mrs. Logan was an active member all her life. Judge Logan did not unite with the church, but gave it his continuing support. He was elected trustee in 1852, and was twice appointed a member of building committees. In 1880 he was named as one of the six trustees of the newly incorporated "The Christian Church of Springfield, Illinois."

✣ ✣ ✣

In the *Millennial Harbinger* of December, 1853, page 716f, appears an obituary of Mr. Hewitt's wife, MRS. LUCILLA H. PAYNE HEWITT, and of his father. The article is not signed but its intimate language leads to the belief that it was written by Josephus Hewitt. It reads:

> Died, of the prevailing epidemic [yellow fever], at the residence of her husband, Mr. J. Hewett, in the city of New Orleans [*Illinois State Journal* says "Natchez"], on Saturday the 22d of October, Mrs. LUCILLA H. HEWETT, daughter of the Rev. William Payne, late of Mason county, Ky., aged 40 years, 1 month, and 4 days. Active in all the relations of a Christian wife, mother, mistress and friend, her loss will be deeply felt wherever she was known. Decidedly practical in her views of life, and its duties, where they required action, no obstacles were sufficient to swerve her from the path which duty indicated. While an afflicted husband and numerous family mourn her loss—to them irreparable—they have the cheering consolation of knowing, that the light of a well-grounded hope illumined her dark pathway to the tomb. She rests from her labors, and her works do follow her.
>
> Also, at the same place, of old age and debility, on Sunday morning, the 30th ult., Mr. THOMAS HEWETT, father of J. Hewett, in the 77th year of his age. For more than sixty-two years the deceased has been a consistent member of the Christian church, having consecrated the dew and freshness of his youth to the service of the Redeemer. He patiently awaited his departure from a world which offered little to attach him to it, save the devoted affection of his off-spring; and when the summons came, the flame of life flickered in the socket for a while, and went out. None could have known his life, or witnessed his death, without exclaiming, "Let me die the death of the righteous, and let my last end be like his."

Alexander Graham

Pastor 1837-1838

BORN: November 29, 1811, at Hartsville, Tennessee
DIED: April 17, 1851, at Marion, Alabama
MARRIED: Mary Cathey, 1836
CHILDREN: None

Herbert Georg Studio

Alexander Graham

Alexander Graham, an early member of the religious movement of Disciples of Christ in middle Tennessee and northern Alabama, became, in his relatively brief career, a meticulous scholar and teacher, a prominent lawyer, and a religious thinker and preacher of uncommon ability.

Graham was born near Hartsville, a small town in Sumner County, Tennessee. He attended the private neighborhood schools intermittently and for a short time studied Greek and Latin with a Dr. Ring of Gallatin, Tennessee.

Graham taught school near his home before his twentieth birthday, and by the age of twenty-four had become proficient in both teaching and in his comprehension of classical education. He was particularly interested in languages, history, and logic. These academic interests were often expressed in poetic and prose compositions; no doubt it was his ability to express himself in poetry that won him his wife, Mary Cathey, in 1836, while he lived in Marion, Alabama.

About the age of eighteen, Graham had become a Baptist under the preaching of an Elder Wiseman, and with Wiseman's encouragement, he shortly thereafter became a preacher. However, in the latter part of 1832 and at the age of twenty-one, while in charge of an academy six miles west of Paris, Tennessee, he became acquainted with the religious views of Alexander Campbell. His intellectual curiosity about Christianity coincided with the emphasis of Campbell's rational religion. He left the Baptists in 1834. That same year he returned to Gallatin, Tennessee, where, in this center of the tobacco country, he, along with a Dr. Anderson and a woman, formed a "congregation" on the principles of the Campbellian reformers. He wrote: "I was once a *worldling,* then a *Baptist;* but I discard every other name but that of *Christ,* of whom I am a Disciple." The little church, called "Electa Cyria," showed the enthusiasm of its founders, for at the end of 1834 there were forty members.

In late 1834, Graham left Tennessee and went to Marion, Alabama. There he met James A. Butler, a preacher of the Disciples of Christ living in the neighboring county of Loundes. He lived with Butler for a year, and in December, 1835, the two moved to Tuscaloosa, the seat of the state government at that time. Here for two years they published a monthly religious periodical called *The Disciple.* They also preached wherever there was an opportunity. In the meantime, Graham had married Mary Cathey.

In the spring of 1837, Graham and his wife left Alabama for Cape Girardeau, Missouri, where he spent the year in charge of an academy, in serious study, and in writing.

He next went to Springfield, Illinois, in the spring of 1837, to become a teacher and the minister of the Christian Church. His editorial interests were continued here, for he published a monthly religious periodical called *The Berean.* The publication existed for one year from January to December, 1838. The articles he wrote for this paper reflect his superior mind and a highly creditable literary style. Graham himself characterized his work in Springfield in *The Berean* as follows:

> The congregation of Disciples in Springfield, now number about ninety members. There has been a gradual increase since its formation, and the first day has never been without its due celebration. I mention this particularly to correct an erroneous report circulated in the neighborhood that this church was dwindling, and would soon go to nothing. There is no religious excitement in this place among any of the churches. Communities have their seasons of apathy and enthusiasm, and although we have had no revival, we have had an accession of 40 members during the last twelve months. It will only require industry and perseverance, to see the truth triumph gloriously.

At the end of 1838 he went back for a visit to Marion, Alabama, his wife's home, and remained there until his death. At the suggestion of his cousin, John P. Graham, a man of social prominence of Marion, he began the study of law. It was not long before he became a lawyer, taking over his cousin's functions of the solicitor's office.

For a decade from 1839 to 1849, Graham gave most of his attention and time to his law practice. He also made several political speeches during this period; his interests, however, were not in politics.

Though the duties of his profession as a lawyer absorbed most of his energy and time, Graham nevertheless continued his linguistic and biblical studies. He read Greek, Latin, and French with facility. His knowledge of Hebrew, German, and Italian increased, and he began the study of Spanish shortly before his death. He preached regularly in the Marion church or made arrangements for others to conduct the services. From a beginning of five members, the church had grown in a few years to a membership of one hundred fifty. In 1846 he had the meetinghouse for the church built at his own expense.

During the decade of his law practice, Graham also took an active part in his community's and state's educational and civic responsibilities. He spoke occasionally on the subject of education and held membership in the Masonic fraternity and the Sons of Temperance. As evidence of his high standing in the Southern states, his portrait was painted by Nicola Marschall, or Mareschal, a celebrated artist of that time, a sketch of whom appears in the National Cyclopedia of American Biography, Volume 17, page 51, c1920. In 1861 Marschall designed the Confederate flag, known as the "Stars and Bars," and the gray uniforms worn by the Confederate soldiers. The portrait of Alexander Graham now in our collection of former pastors of First Christian Church is made from a photograph of this painting by Nicola Marschall, which now hangs in the Department of Archives and History of the State of Alabama at Montgomery, Alabama.[1]

---

[1]About 1859 Marschall painted a portrait of Alexander Campbell with a beard, which hangs in the library of Christian Theological Seminary at Butler University in Indianapolis, Indiana.

In 1849 Graham turned to his first main interest, education. He abandoned his law practice and became president of the Marion Female Seminary. The future was bright and the only thing that seemed able to stop the creative endeavors of this young and strong-willed man would be death. This came on April 17, 1851, after a short illness.

In the *Millennial Harbinger* of June, 1851, on page 359, Alexander Campbell wrote:

> I sympathize with the relatives, friends, and brethren of our deceased Bro. Graham, in their irreparable loss, and regret that the narrative of the remarkable and eventful life of this much gifted brother, communicated by our Bro. P. B. Lawson, is . . . reluctantly, but necessarily, excluded from our pages. A. C.

After the death of Alexander Graham, MRS. MARY CATHEY GRAHAM married Pope Massey, and after Mr. Massey's death she married Arnold Jolly. There were no children of any of these marriages. This information is contained in a letter written by Blanche Graham (a niece of Alexander Graham) to Mary R. Moseley of Tuscaloosa, Alabama, October 20, 1952. As of the time of writing, Miss Graham was past 80 years of age.

Jeremiah P. Lancaster

Pastor 1842-1843

BORN: No information
DIED: No information
MARRIED: No information

In Judge Charles P. Kane's *The Christian Church of Springfield . . . During the First Sixty Years,* page 12, appears the following:

> The following year (1842) occurred the second Annual Meeting held at Springfield. The bright, particular star at this convention was Jerry P. Lancaster of Missouri. As a pulpit orator he was probably surpassed only by Josephus Hewett among our early preachers in Illinois. He was a man of limited education but of fine natural endowments and the master of a native eloquence that swayed his listeners at will. Such was his impressiveness that one who heard him said, fifty years afterward, he could give a complete outline of the sermon. The Springfield church was so delighted with him, they pressed him into service as their third pastor. He remained but a year, however, being decoyed away by the superior persuasiveness of our Jacksonville Central Church brethren; thence in 1844 he removed to Dubuque, Iowa, at the invitation of our Brother Mobley, who had changed his residence to that city. William and Lavina Lavely united with the church during Mr. Lancaster's ministry.

The Illinois Legislature was in session during the early months of 1843, and the Protestant ministers of Springfield were called upon to take turns serving as chaplains of the two houses. The *Illinois Journal* reports that Mr. Lancaster offered prayer at the opening sessions of the Senate on January 5, 15, and 24, and on February 2, 1843.

During much of the nineteenth century many ministers of the Disciples engaged in hundreds of debates with ministers of other denominations or sects. Alexander Campbell was the foremost. Shortly before Jeremiah P. Lancaster came to Springfield, he took part in a debate on baptism with B. R. Johnson of the Methodist Episcopal Church. It was probably one of the first of such debates to be printed, and deserves recognition here. The printed debate is in the library of the Christian Theological Seminary at Butler University. It was printed by Robinson and Williams, Boonville, Missouri, 1842. On October 27, 1841, and some days following, the debate took place at Fayette, Missouri, on the following questions:

1. Are infants proper subjects of baptism?
2. Is immersion essential to the ordinance of baptism?
3. Does baptism form a condition or part of a condition of justification, pardon, and remission of sins?
4. Does baptism as an emblem, refer to the baptism of the Holy Ghost or grace of regeneration; or to the burial and resurrection of Jesus Christ?

In the printed book are "Certificates" indicating that each speaker was a bona fide representative of the religious body for whom he spoke and to which he belonged, as follows:

1. We, the undersigned, members and preachers of the Methodist Episcopal Church, certify that we believe Benjamin R. Johnson well qualified to conduct the argument for the church to which we belong, in the debate between Jeremiah P. Lancaster and himself.

[Signed by eleven names.]

2. We, the undersigned, Teachers of the Christian Religion and Proclaimers of the Gospel, do regard Elder J. P. Lancaster as a gentleman and a Christian, and are willing to risk him in a debate, in defence of the truths of our holy religion, with any men who may be selected by any of the parties or sects of the present age.

Signed by:

Henry Thomas
Allen Wright
Joel H. Hayden
Levi Vancamp
F. R. Palmer
T. N. Gaines
A. H. F. Payne
S. P. Johnson
Dick Young
H. L. Boon
Thomas M. Allen
M. P. Wills

The rules provided that each speaker should speak 30 minutes without interruption "unless he is pleased to waive his right." King James' version of the Bible was used as authority. There were three moderators, one selected by each side, who in turn chose "a third person, who belonged to neither party, for the purpose of keeping order, and the speakers to the question."

Who won? Undoubtedly the partisans of each side claimed the victory.

There is an unfortunate and dramatic sequel to Lancaster's work as a minister of the gospel, as recorded by T. P. Haley.[1]

JERRY P. LANCASTER

Of the ministers who labored in an early day in Clay county, no one is more frequently mentioned than Jerry P. Lancaster, who immersed Moses E. Lard, and to whom General A. W. Doniphan refers in his letter.

This distinguished preacher was from Kentucky and in an early day, was a Methodist preacher. He came into the Christian church, it is thought, in Anderson county, Kentucky, and perhaps at Lawrenceburg. He came to Missouri in an early day, and is mentioned in the journal of Elder T. M. Allen, as early as the year 1840. While a resident of Missouri, his home was in the eastern part of the State, perhaps in Pike county. He labored with others, in Monroe, Marion and Ralls, in Boone, Howard and Calloway, and made an occasional visit to the upper counties of the State, preaching in Lexington, Independence, Richmond, Liberty and Salem, in Platee county. In all these places he is remembered as an eloquent preacher of the gospel. He was remarkably successful in revival efforts, and baptized great numbers.

It is recorded that he, at one time [1841] held a debate with a Methodist minister, in Fayette, Missouri, the Rev. Ben R. Johnson. The baptismal question was of course disputed. I have often heard it related that during the discussion the Rev. Mr. Johnson undertook to depreciate the ability of Alexander Campbell. In reply, Mr. Lancaster said. "Mr. Moderator, if one of Alexander Campbell's ideas should happen to get into my friend's head, it would burst like a bomb-shell."

In the year 1849, this brilliant man began to give evidence that he had fallen away from his faith in Christ. . . . He emigrated with that great throng, in that year, to the gold fields of California. Evil reports came back concerning his conduct on the way, and while in that far off land he made complete shipwreck of his faith, and was known as a bad man. Some years later he returned to Missouri. On his way home he was taken severely sick at Panama, and was prostrate for

---

[1]Haley, T P., *Historical and Biographical Sketches of the Early Churches and Pioneer Preachers of the Christian Church in Missouri* (St. Louis: Christian Publishing Co., 1888) pp. 338-341.

many months. But for the kindness of his Masonic brethren, he would have died of utter want and neglect, but they kindly cared for him during his illness, and helped him on his way home. He reached home utterly broken in health, and profoundly penitent for all his sins. He began at once to attend the meetings of the church, perhaps in New London, Ralls county. On one occasion brother T. M. Allen, who had known him well, when he was a worthy minister of the gospel, was holding a meeting there. He attended the meeting. At the close of one of the services, he approached brother Allen, and asked an interview. This kindhearted man, in the sternest manner, said to him: "Jerry, I have heard that you have denied the blessed Lord who redeemed you, and whom you once preached, and that you are an infidel, and if this is true, I want nothing to do with you." The fallen preacher burst into tears, and said: "I have indeed done wickedly, but my faith is as strong as it ever was. I must talk with you." The interview was granted. . . . The result was, that before the meeting closed, he asked the church to allow him to make a statement. He said: "Brethren, you have heard much about my wicked conduct, perhaps much that is untrue, but perhaps the worst, you have heard, is not as bad as I have really done. I have been a great sinner, but God has led me through a long and sore affliction to see the enormity of my sins. I do not make this confession nor this statement with the hope of being reinstated in the church of which I was once an honored member, in which I was a preacher, and which I still love, but I have made it because I could not be happy without making it. I have asked God to forgive me. I hope He has done so. I do not ask you to forgive me now, but I do ask that you will keep watch over me, and if, by the help of God I can so live as to regain your confidence, then forgive me. I do not ask to be taken back into the church now, perhaps it will never be best to do that, but I do want to linger about the courts of the Lord, that I may have your prayers and watchful care." The effect of such a speech can readily be imagined. Good men and women wept for him, and freely promised all he had asked. It was not long till he was restored to the fellowship of the church in which he died, but never afterwards exercised the functions of his sacred office. The evening of his life was spent in the practice of law. . . .

Of his family I have no information. Whether he left children or not I am not advised. He immersed M. E. Lard who, to the day of his death, spoke of him in terms of tenderness.

William M. Brown

Pastor 1843-1847

BORN: Kentucky
DIED: November 22, 1863, at Springfield, Illinois
MARRIED: Julia A. ———

This man was a striking personality. He was six feet two inches in height and of fine form, weighing two hundred pounds. His head was large, his face strong and clean-shaven, and his dark hair he wore long for a male, and decidedly pompadour.

He came to Springfield in 1841 and was pastor of the church there [in 1843—1847].

He was elected as the first president of Eureka College [in 1855-1856], but his service was only nominal.

His chief work was that of an evangelist. In this sphere he was probably the most noted among the Disciples during his period of service in Illinois. He was regarded as a powerful preacher. His sermons united argument with impassioned appeal. In dealing with what he considered denominational doctrinal errors he was often as inexorable as logic could be. . . . On one such occasion, a woman auditor, not in sympathy with all his teachings, personally expressed the wish that she "might have his scalp for a scrub-brush." At one of the earlier State Meetings held in Springfield, the mountain-top was reached on the Lord's Day. It was the custom then, at the close of the communion, to shake hands throughout the assembly. Some of the elder brethren would embrace each other and weep tears of joy. On this occasion, . . . the gentle Barton W. Stone . . . cried out: "Brother Brown, you speak too harshly of people's errors. Dear brother, when you find a stone across the path of truth, just carefully roll it away, but don't try to spat the man who laid it there." . . . To his aggressiveness he added a brilliant imagination. His pictures of heavenly things were sublime. Great crowds attended his meetings and many were turned to the Lord. After all, a sweet tenderness was in his soul. . . .

The churches at Springfield, Bloomington, Pittsfield, and at many other places in the State, are yet much indebted to this great preacher.[1]

William M. Brown is named as one of the incorporators of Eureka College in a special charter which was granted by the legislature of Illinois by an act approved February 6, 1855. The institution had previously been known as Walnut Grove Academy. In September, 1855, it was opened as Eureka College with Elder William M. Brown as its first president. He and Elder William Davenport were appointed solicitors for

---

[1]Nathaniel S. Haynes, *History of the Disciples of Christ in Illinois, 1819-1914* (Cincinnati: Standard Publishing Company, 1915), pp. 485-486.

the college. They visited localities in Illinois and adjoining states to canvass for students and donations. In a few months they reported over $60,000 in subscriptions.

The following letter by Mr. Brown to Barton W. Stone tells of his evangelistic work at Springfield before becoming pastor here:

Jacksonville, Illinois: August 11, 1841.

Dear Father Stone:

Brother Patton and myself arrived in Springfield July 3, and commenced a meeting, which continued four weeks during which we had 75 valuable additions in the city and vicinity. May the good Lord bless them, and save them in His everlasting Kingdom.

W. M. Brown[2]

The success of William M. Brown as an evangelist is evidenced by letters from him published in the *Millennial Harbinger,* edited by Alexander Campbell. In the volume of 1846 is the following:

Frankfort, Ky., April 15, 1846.

My year's labors as an evangelist in the Mason county co-operation, terminated on the 1st of this month. During the year I preached 334 regular discourses and immersed 176 persons. The preaching, I suppose, was about half the services rendered. . . .

W. M. Brown

In the volume of 1855, page 54, appears:

ILLINOIS—Bro. W. M. Brown, of Pittsfield, September 9th, writes: "A few days since we closed a meeting in this place with 64 additions. Among the number were Methodists, Congregationalists, and Baptists. A Baptist minister (Bro. Chapman) was among the valuable accessions. He delivered us a short but appropriate address, stating his reasons for leaving the Baptists and uniting with us on the Bible alone."

The Illinois State Archives disclose that he became chaplain of the Thirty-eighth Illinois Volunteer Infantry in the Civil War. He was mustered in on May 28, 1863, at Newton, Illinois.

[2]From *The Christian Messenger,* conducted by Barton W. Stone, August, 1841, Vol. 11, No. 12, pp. 416-417.

At the battle of Chickamauga (September 19-23, 1863) he contracted a cold and died November 22, 1863, at Springfield, Illinois.

✣ ✣ ✣

In the library of the Disciples Divinity House at Chicago is a complete series of bound volumes of the *Millennial Harbinger,* at least part of which had been in the library of William M. Brown. This is indicated by a bookplate in some of the earliest volumes, reading as follows:

> CHRISTIAN CHURCH LIBRARY
>
> ---
>
> No books to be taken from the church
>
> ---
>
> Donated by Mrs. Julia A. Brown from the Library of her husband, the late Elder Wm. M. Brown

It is likely that the Christian Church library referred to in the bookplate is that of this congregation, inasmuch as the Browns lived in Springfield for some years. However, this is only a conjecture.

We have no further information about MRS. JULIA A. BROWN.

Andrew Jackson Kane

Pastor 1847-1851

BORN: February 11, 1817, in Guilford County, North Carolina
DIED: November 14, 1896, at Springfield, Illinois
MARRIED: Caroline Maria Beers, May 13, 1847
CHILDREN: Martha Kane (Mrs. Thomas DeQuincy Tully)
Charles P. Kane (County Judge of Sangamon County, 1892-1896)
Julia Elena Kane
Isabel Kane
Eugene Stillman Kane
Henry Beers Kane
Newell Kane
Jenny Coleman Kane } Died in infancy
Caroline Kane }
Wilbur Kane }

Herbert Georg Studio

Andrew Jackson Kane

Herbert Georg Studio

Caroline Maria Beers Kane

Andrew Jackson Kane was the only member of this congregation who later became its pastor, serving from 1847-1851. He was widely known as Elder A. J. Kane, because Disciple ministers of that period objected to being called "Reverend," preferring the title "Elder." His work as a minister covered much of the state, and he took an active part in the organization of the American Missionary Society and of the Illinois Christian Missionary convention. He was selected to preach the sermon at the dedication of the new church building at Fifth and Jackson Streets on February 12, 1882, when Joseph Buford Allen was pastor.

Andrew J. Kane . . . was left an orphan in infancy and in his early boyhood was taken by his oldest brother, Morrison Kane, to Indiana, where he was reared. At the age of twenty-one, Andrew started out in life for himself, going to Illinois. Not pleased with the outlook of Chicago, then an uninviting village half sunken in the mire, he came to Peoria and afterward to Springfield, which city was the place of his residence until his death, with the exception of a brief period of about three years from 1851 to 1854 [at which time he was pastor of the Jacksonville Christian Church]. Arriving in the vicinity of Springfield in 1839, he assisted in building the first bridge across the Sangamon River [at Carpenter's mill].

Having united with the Christian Church at Indianapolis under the preaching of John O'Kane in 1836, Andrew connected himself at once with the congregation in his home town (Springfield). Urged by the brethren, he decided to enter the ministry and to this end took up the study of Hebrew, Latin, Greek and English literature under private tutors. . . . In 1842, he was ordained to preach by the Christian congregation at Springfield.

His field was central Illinois, though at times he passed the boundaries of the State. Before the age of railways and telegraphs in the sparsely settled country, where few pastors were permanently employed, he preached continuously, riding on horseback to various towns with his saddlebags behind him. In one side was his Bible and in the other his necessary articles of wearing apparel. No name was better known than his, no views more widely heard in those early days for the development and settlement of Illinois. Meetings were held, churches organized, infant congregations cared for, and occasionally an encounter was had with some champion of the opposition in public debate. Some of his evangelistic meetings were marvelously successful for the times and his converts numbered thousands.

Of his ability as a preacher the testimony is manifold and abundant. Bailey D. Dawson, of Chicago, formerly of Jacksonville, Illinois, . . . says: "Through many successful years, by his excellent good sense, clever practical gospel preaching, his exemplary Christian walk and conversation, he won many precious souls to Christ and achieved an enviable name as a good pastor—the ablest minister this church ever had then or in later times."[1]

In the *Millennial Harbinger* of 1847 appears:

Fort Madison, I. T., February 15, 1847.

Brother Kain [Kane], of Springfield, Illinois, was over with us lately. He spoke eleven or twelve nights (including Lord's day) in succession, to crowded audiences, in our court-house. Ten persons came forward and obeyed the gospel, and three were added to our congregation by letter. We had to cut through ice over one foot thick to immerse during our meeting. Wm. Leslie.

In the *Millennial Harbinger* of 1848 is the following:

ANOTHER TROPHY OF THE LEXINGTON DEBATE

Springfield, Illinois, March 30, 1848.

In the fall of 1845, I commenced preaching in the town of Macomb, M'Donough county, Illinois, in company with brother Isaac Murphy, now of Bethany, Va. We organized a congregation of about seventeen members, to which were added some twenty-seven or eight during the same meeting. Since that time I have visited them occasionally, and the congregation has increased to 75 or 80 members. Among them is a very amiable sister, the wife of brother B. Naylor, who was convinced by the "Campbell and Rice Debate." She was a devoted Presbyterian for some time; but having heard her husband read the Debate in the family, during his leisure hours, she yielded to the power of truth, renounced infant sprinkling, and obeyed the gospel understandingly and for herself.

A. J. Kane

[1]From an article by Thomas T. Holton (Pastor 1868-1870), printed in *Past and Present of the City of Springfield and Sangamon County Illinois,* by Joseph Wallace, Chicago. The J. S. Clarke Publishing Company, 1904, Volume 1, pages 419-421.

In 1853 Alexander Campbell visited various Illinois churches, trying to raise money to endow a chair of chemistry at Bethany College. He spent some time at Jacksonville, Illinois. A. J. Kane was then pastor of the Jacksonville Christian Church, but left to resume his duties as pastor of First Christian Church in Springfield. In "Notes on a Tour to Illinois," in the *Millennial Harbinger* of December, 1853, Mr. Campbell said:

> . . . Bro. Kane was obliged to give the parting hand at Jacksonville, and attend to his pastoral duties. My loss of his aid will, no doubt, be a gain to the cause which he so ably and faithfully sustains in his own proper field of labor. We want a hundred such men in this great State of Illinois.

Elder A. P. Cobb, who delivered the address at his funeral, said: "He was a reasoner rather than an exhorter, a natural theologian—a preacher to preachers. He would have graced and filled the chair of the Bible in any of our colleges."

❖ ❖ ❖

MRS. CAROLINE MARIA BEERS KANE was born February 20, 1827, at Springfield, Illinois, and died October 30, 1912, at Springfield, Illinois. She was the daughter of Philo and Martha Stillman Beers. Her parents' marriage was the "wedding of the first white couple in the territory which afterward became the county of Sangamon." It is described in detail by Judge Charles P. Kane, grandson, in a lecture read before the Illinois State Historical Society on January 25, 1906. At this wedding the family borrowed all the white flour in the neighborhood but could not get enough for a suitable wedding cake. They then prepared a cake of cornmeal covered with white icing. It presented a sufficiently "festal appearance," but there was merry disillusionment when it was cut. The minister, Rev. Stephen England, had only well-worn Indian moccasins for footwear and had to borrow a pair of leather shoes from his brother-in-law, Evan Brittin, in which to officiate. (Exactly 61 years later, on November 2, 1881, Flora, a granddaughter of Evan Brittin, became the wife of Charles Philo Kane, grandson of Philo Beers.)

Philo and Martha Beers were charter members of the original congregation in 1833. Their daughter Caroline was then 6 years old. Later she united with the church and became the wife of Andrew Jackson Kane on May 13, 1847. She was an active and devoted member of the church until her death and was prominent in the social and religious life of the city and in the Daughters of the American Revolution. She was described as a woman of superior intelligence and strong character.

She was chosen to turn the first spadeful of dirt on June 4, 1911, at the ground-breaking ceremony for the erection of the present church building.

The Kanes had ten children, of whom seven grew to maturity and became active members of the congregation. Through Caroline Maria Beers Kane there has been a continuous line of membership in this congregation through five generations:

(1) Philo Beers and Martha Stillman Beers (charter members), parents of:
(2) Caroline Beers Kane, mother of:
(3) Charles Philo Kane, father of:
(4) Caroline Kane (Mrs. C. Hubert Streiff)[2]
(4) Elizabeth Kane (Mrs. O. L. Zelle), and
(4) Philo Beers Kane,[2] father of:
(5) Barbara Mae Kane[2] and
(5) Vancil York Kane[2]

[2]Present members.

John H. Hughes

Pastor 1851-1852

BORN: No information
DIED: At San Jose, California
MARRIED: No information

Herbert Georg Studio

John H. Hughes

According to news notes in the *Illinois Journal,* of Springfield, John H. Hughes performed a remarkably large number of marriages while he was pastor of this church. He was chaplain of Springfield Masonic Lodge No. 4 in 1854. In the *Illinois Journal* of October 5, 1854, is a list of the Grand Officers of the Grand Lodge of Illinois, A. F. & A. M., in which he is named as Grand Chaplain.

After leaving this church, Mr. Hughes became pastor of various Christian Churches in Missouri, including those at St. Joseph and Kansas City. The minutes of various Missouri Conventions give J. H. Hughes of Kansas City, Missouri, as recording secretary of the Missouri Christian Convention in 1886-1887. He was president of the Convention in 1888-1889. He was included in the first list of ministers in the Missouri minutes (1889), but not afterward. In *The History of the Warrensburg [Missouri] Christian Church, 1855-1928,* by Virginia Gilkerson Hedges, we read:

> J. H. Hughes followed next (after J. H. Foy was called to St. Louis). He was the type of a lawyer and plead each case, in love of both God and man. He was very successful in gaining converts. He died some years ago in San José, California. It was said that no other man at that time could claim more souls for his hire.

In Volume 3 of *The Missouri Christian Lectureship* for 1884-1885, the Foreword states that J. H. Hughes was Chairman of the Executive Committee of the Lectureship.

Alexander Johnson

Pastor 1852-1854

BORN: No information
DIED: No information
MARRIED: Name not known
CHILDREN: Four daughters
One son

We find various references to Alexander "Johnson" and to Alexander "Johnston," which lead us to believe that they are the same man, who served as our pastor in 1852-1854. He later became the first pastor of the Main Street Christian Church at New Castle, Indiana, from August, 1863, to February, 1866, during the building and completion of its first church edifice. Not much is known of his other labors in this part of the country, but considerable is known of his career in the far west.

We quote from E. B. Ware's *History of the Disciples of Christ in California,* published at Healdsburg, California, in 1916.

CHRISTIAN COLLEGE.

In 1869 Alexander Johnston came to the state of California with his wife and family of four daughters and a son. Johnston was a man of fine appearance, well educated, and a fine preacher. In fact, along the line of "first principles" he had few equals. He was a college-bred man, and at once took a leading place in the educational forces of the State among our people.

Johnston stopped at Woodland a little while, then came to Napa and looked the field over with the view of founding a school, but finally located at Santa Rosa. He began to preach for the church, and immediately began to talk up the matter of founding a Christian school in that fertile country and growing town. The country then was new, and the public schools were poor. The State University was then only on paper, and the people were anxious for better educational facilities.

Hesperian College at Woodland held the priority of age and of claim upon the brotherhod of the State for financial support and for patronage. It had been struggling for over ten years to get its head above the water, but the Santa Rosa movement found supporters. Reverend Johnston had a wonderful faculty for rallying men to his enterprises, of forming quick combinations and carrying them into immediate execution. His faculty for a long and continuous administration of plans which he set on foot was not so good.

At the State meeting at Woodland in 1870, as has been stated, a new paper, the *Bible Expositor,* was started. Johnston was made editor. This gave him prestige, and on January 1, 1871, the first number of the new paper appeared.

Soon after this Johnston began the active work of founding a college at Santa Rosa. A fine plot of ground was secured at the head of B street, and a splendid two-story building erected thereon, with all the necessary equipment. On September 23, 1872, the doors of Christian College were opened to the public. The Honorable T. H. Laine of San José, a stepson of Thomas Thompson, delivered the opening address. The head of the faculty was Alexander Johnston, A.M., Professor of Hebrew, Mental and Moral Philosophy; Harrison Price, A.B., Professor of Latin and Greek Language and Literature; A. M. Merriman, Professor of Mathematics, and Florence G. Johnston, M.A., teacher of music. Johnston continued in the school about two years, when difficulties arose, and he resigned.

The college flourished for only a few years, and then the property was sold and became Ursuline Academy.

Among Johnston's converts in California was no less a person that Edwin Markham, the poet, author of "The Man with the Hoe." In Stidger's biography of *Edwin Markham,* the poet gives a pen picture of the minister, spelling the name "Johnson." He also mentions that the poet's mother was a member of the brotherhood of Disciples of Christ, and states that he also became a member and was immersed.[1]

Said the poet on that unforgettable evening: "My mother was a Roman matron, a woman of power, one who could have led an army to battle, but she was also a thoughtful woman with a strong slant toward religion.

. . . .

"She was a seeker after religious truth always and took me with her, even as a mere child, on these religious quests. She belonged to the Campbellite Church, known now as the Disciples. There was just enough controversy and clash of wits in that early church to satisfy her keen and vivid intelligence. In those days the Disciples specialized in Bible lore, and what was not known to them of immersion as the true form of baptism was not known to any group on earth.

"I remember that now and then my mother would dress me and take me to what were called 'revival meetings' or 'protracted meetings,'

[1]William L. Stidger, *Edwin Markham* (Nashville: The Abingdon Press, 1933), pp. 226-229.

where all the celebrities of the church came, each of them dowered with immense beards and broad-bottomed physical bodies; preachers with voices like the seven thunders of Patmos; voices that could and did hurl thunderbolts of the fear of God into the most abject sinners.

. . . .

"Among the great preachers of that church in those early days was Alexander Johnson, a tall, thin, wiry personality, with broad clifflike brows; long, skinny fingers like the talons of a vulture, and whenever he walked across the floor of a church toward the pulpit he was the target of all eyes. He was a thoughtful man, crammed with Bible quotations and always ended his sermons with a terrific appeal to the terrors of the law.

"We all sat there, especially the children, pale and horrified with the prospect of a gulf of hell into which we might soon be hurled. In those days there was not so much 'sweetness and light' in preaching. Those preachers seemed to be terribly in earnest. They had what Goethe called 'an inner earnestness' in their preaching, looking upon life and religion as a most serious business.

. . . .

"I joined the church and was immersed in San José, California. I was immersed in a deep pool outside of the town somewhere. I took the matter seriously, and, while I don't look upon baptism with quite the intensity of those early brethren, still I look upon religion with the same seriousness that I always did. I know that the truly religious man is the only man who has founded his life on reason and Christ."

B. F. Perky

Pastor 1854-1856

BORN: No information
DIED: No information
MARRIED: } (Wife and children are mentioned by Mr.
CHILDREN: } Perky, but no names or dates are given.)

B. F. Perky became a leading figure in the churches of Disciples of Christ of Ohio, and is mentioned favorably three times in Henry K. Shaw's *Buckeye Disciples.* He was an evangelist of the Ohio convention.

Alexander Campbell, in the *Millennial Harbinger* of February, 1853, said of him:

A SPECIAL PROVIDENCE.

I congratulate, not only the beloved Bro. Perky, on his remarkable recovery from the loss of reason, as the consequence of physical derangement of a very peculiar character, but also his family, and all the brethren in Ohio that knew him, admired him, and loved him, and they are not a few. Their prayers have been heard and answered, and he is himself again.

I heard Bro. Perky at four great meetings on the Western Reserve, in 1851, with the greatest satisfaction and delight. I regarded him as a great master-spirit in the midst of a great congregation, and in the same ratio I was afflicted in his affliction, and grieved at what I fearfully anticipated a great loss to his family and friends, and to the cause of our Great Redeemer. But the Lord has been very merciful to him and to the people, in his truly remarkable restoration. His disease was purely physical in its incipiency and general character; but its seat being in the head, suddenly involved the brain, and deprived him of all its healthy functions, so that his mind and body were, for months, a perfect wreck. But by the science, the skill, and the care of the officers and superintendents of the Ohio State Asylum, and especially by the grace and mercy of God, he has been restored. How true the Sunday School verse:

A fever or a blow may shake
Our wisdom's boasted rule,
And of the brightest genius make
A madman or a fool.

The following narrative will afford such interest and information as will more than pay for the space which it occupies and the time spent in reading it. A. C.

Newton Falls, O., January 19, 1853.

My Venerable Brother: Permit me to say to you, and, through the Harbinger, to many anxious friends, that, in the good Providence of God, I am restored to my full measure of physical and mental health, and hail, with inexpressible delight and gratitude, the privilege of mingling with my brethren once more in the social circles and in the great congregation. . . .

It is with heartfelt satisfaction and profound gratitude I record the fact, that during my long separation from my family, their wants were kindly cared for by the brotherhood from Allegheny City, Pa., to Ashland, Ohio. The "cruse of oil and barrel of meal" were not allowed to become exhausted during a protracted illness of nearly one year. In addition to material aid from numerous congregations and individuals, letters of condolence and sympathy, emanating from the purest hearts and ablest pens, besides visits in person from those who knew how to sympathize with the sorely stricken, contributed much towards mitigating the sorrows of my deeply afflicted companion and children, and the perpetuation of the life of the best of wives, and the most tender and prudent of mothers. . . .

My wife sends much love to Sister Campbell. With much affection, I have the honor to be your brother in tribulation, and in the kingdom and patience of Jesus Christ, and in the hope of Israel.

B. F. Perky.

B. F. Perky became pastor of the Christian Church at Springfield early in 1856 after having preached at the church several times. After a few months the elders of the church waited upon him and advised him that "such was the opposition to his further continuance as pastor that his services could no longer be profitable, and in their judgment, ought to cease." Already there had been some misunderstanding between Mr. Perky and certain members of the church. He then accused the congregation of violating a compact and doing him great injury. Without consulting the elders or the congregation, he mailed a circular to the Christian ministers of the state calling on them to meet in Springfield "to consider questions of great importance." In January, 1857, forty-two preachers responded, and listened to Mr. Perky's side of the case. Mr. Perky prepared a circular, which is in the Illinois State Historical Library setting forth his version. The meeting of the ministers issued what they called a "Decision" in which they held that "the church at Springfield has done him a palpable injury by violating the solemn compact and should make reparation." The congregation appointed a committee, whose report was made to the church and adopted by it February 8, 1857. In Haynes' History, it is said: "This report bears the unmistakable stamp of that master-mind, A. J. Kane." The report is as follows:

CHRISTIAN MEETING-HOUSE, SPRINGFIELD, FEB. 8, 1857.

At a meeting of the congregation in Springfield, Feb. 8, 1857, the following report was read and adopted:

"WHEREAS, Jonathan Atkinson, Theophilus Sweet, E. W. Bakewell and I. N. Carman, the majority of a committee appointed by the late Preachers' Convention held in this city, have presented the elders of this church with a copy of what they style their 'decision,' in which, among other things, they assume to decide as follows:

" 'The grievances of Bro. Perkey are great. The church at Springfield has done him a palpable injury by violating a solemn compact, and justice and love alike bind them to make reparation, as far as possible, for the injury, pecuniary and otherwise, sustained by him and the cause of our Lord Jesus Christ.'

"And, WHEREAS, The investigation of said grievances (as they term it) was altogether partial and *ex parte,* insomuch as they only heard his statement, and such evidence as he saw fit to produce, and did not receive or seek any other, although informed that they could have any information in possession of the elders in relation to matters properly submitted to said committee, nor was the church permitted to select any part of the tribunal;

"Therefore, *Resolved,* That we utterly repudiate and deny the authority arrogated by said committee to try this church or to pass any decision on its action.

"*Resolved,* That a church properly organized is responsible to no tribunal on earth, except to the civil law in cases under its cognizance, and that we regard this action of the committee as an assumption of power, unwarranted by the word of God or the practice of the Christian Church, and a bold attempt to lord it over the heritage of God.

"*Resolved,* That when this church feels itself incompetent to manage its temporal and spiritual affairs, and deems it necessary to have assistance, it not only has the right, but claims the right, to choose a part, at least, of the tribunal to which matters may be properly submitted.

"*Resolved,* That the statement of said committee that 'the church in Springfield has done him a palpable wrong by violating a solemn compact,' is reckless and without foundation.

"*Resolved,* That this church approves the action of the elders in communicating to Elder Perkey 'that such was the opposition to his further continuance as pastor of the congregation, that his services could be no longer profitable and, in their judgment, ought to cease,' and we believe it was done with the best of motives for his good, and for the interest of the cause of Christ.

"*Resolved,* That the church holds itself amenable to no Conference, Synod or Convention, claiming the exclusive right to control its own private and public concerns, but willing and desirous to co-operate with others in promoting the great cause of religion as long as such right is conceded.

"*Resolved,* That while we are disposed to respect the brethren composing the committee, as ministers and proclaimers of the gospel, so long as they confine their operations to the legitimate work to which they are called, we must most decidedly, in the fear of God and in all Christian forbearance, utterly repudiate and set at naught the so-called decision so far as it relates to this church.

"(Signed) A. J. Kane,
"Richard Latham,
"Joseph Bennett,
"A. C. Constant,
"*Committee.*"

Despite A. J. Kane's outspoken opposition to the action of the Preachers' Convention, it appears that he had a rather high opinion of Mr. Perky personally, as evidenced by a letter quoted by Mr. Perky in his Circular as follows:

Springfield, Dec. 3d, 1856.

To All the Brethren in Christ:—This is to certify that the bearer, Bro. B. F. Perky, has been sojourning and laboring with us for some time very acceptably, and being about to leave, it affords me much pleasure to state that we have found in him a man true and faithful—the Christian and the gentleman. Any attention shown him on your part, will be supporting the cause of our common Master and gratefully acknowledged by your brother in Christ.

A. J. Kane

This controversy has had a historical significance to the entire brotherhood of Disciples of Christ. It tended to establish firmly the status of an individual congregation as being wholly independent in the conduct of its own congregational affairs—not subject to the control or dictation of any so-called supervising authority such as a "conference, synod or convention." The stand thus taken by Elder A. J. Kane and his colleagues appears to be generally accepted, not only in Illinois but throughout the entire brotherhood of Disciples of Christ.

Calling attention to the refusal of the 1961 Kansas City Assembly of the International Convention to override historic congregational polity when it disapproved a resolution calling for immediate steps toward desegregation of National City Christian Church, Howard E. Short, editor of *The Christian,* has said that current views on this subject seem to remain the same.

The Illinois State Historical Library has a copy of the circular, evidently sent out by Mr. Perky from Mount Pleasant, Iowa, in 1857, to David King, Jacksonville, Illinois. It contains two letters: one from M. Berkey and Wm. London, Mount Pleasant, Iowa, July 29th, 1857, to Elder B. F. Perky regarding matters pertaining to the Christian church at Springfield, Illinois, and the Preachers' Convention held there in January, 1857; and the other his reply, giving his account of the misunderstanding, referred to by Haynes.

Sterling Elwood Pearre

Pastor 1856-1862

BORN: August 27, 1825, in Clermont County, Ohio
DIED: January 9, 1904, at California, Missouri
MARRIED: (1) Name unknown
Children: Names and number unknown
(2) Angelina Carman
Children: Henrietta Lockwood Pearre
(Mrs. Edmund Wilkes)
Daughter: Name unknown
(3) Caroline Neville
Children: None

Herbert Georg Studio

Sterling Elwood Pearre

Herbert Georg Studio

Caroline Neville Pearre

THE PEARRE FAMILY

By Edmund Wilkes, Jr.[1]

According to a notation in an old Bible, in the handwriting of Henrietta Lockwood Pearre Wilkes (my mother—wife of Elder Edmund Wilkes), her father, Dr. Sterling Elwood Pearre, was born August 27, 1825, in Clermont County, Ohio. His parents were Otho and Melissa Penick Bagby Pearre of Kentucky.

He first became a physician and surgeon. He was known as an eclectic doctor, which school of medicine taught the use of plant extracts instead of minerals as medicine. Dr. Pearre became an expert botanist, and was acquainted with a number of the leading botanists of his day. He made a collection of unusual plant specimens, pressed in a large book which he called his Herbarium.

It was while he was practicing medicine that Dr. Pearre decided to become a Christian minister. He was practicing medicine in either Pennsylvania or Kentucky at the time of an epidemic of yellow fever, which was a common scourge in those days, and his wife and all his children died from it. It is said that he quit the practice of medicine because his medical knowledge and skill were insufficient to save his own wife and family.

Alexander Campbell induced him to attend Bethany College in Virginia. He graduated with honors, and devoted his full time to the ministry, serving many of the prominent churches of Disciples of Christ. In 1857-1858 S. E. Pearre, M.D., was assistant professor at Eureka College.

---

[1]Edmund Wilkes, Jr., who resides at 4449 South Benton Avenue, Kansas City 30, Missouri, is a grandson of two of the pastors of First Christian Church. His father, Edmund Wilkes, a minister, was the son of Lanceford Bramblett Wilkes, pastor in 1866-1868. His mother was Henrietta Pearre, daughter of Dr. Sterling Elwood Pearre (pastor in 1856-1862) and Angelina Carman Pearre.

The research by Mr. Wilkes in regard to the details of the lives of his two grandfathers and their families appears to be more thorough than anything we have observed in print. We are glad, therefore, to make use of his labors.—Ed. (See also L. B. Wilkes, 92.)

Dr. Pearre's second wife was Angelina Carman, a quite energetic woman who died in 1862, leaving one daughter, Henrietta (Nettie) Lockwood Pearre, then five years old. At the age of twelve, Nettie became a student at Christian College in Columbia, Missouri, and lived there most of the time until she graduated, after which she was employed as a member of the faculty until she married father, Reverend Edmund Wilkes, son of Reverend and Mrs. Lanceford Bramblett Wilkes, and became my mother.

One of the members of the faculty at Christian College while Nettie was a student there was a gifted young woman, Caroline Neville, who became Dr. Pearre's third wife. Caroline went to Lexington, Kentucky, to visit her brother at one time when Dr. Pearre came there to hold a revival meeting. She considered him the most intellectual man she had ever met, and they fell in love and were married.

I understand that he always had been a shy, sensitive man, of scholarly attainments with the ability to rise to eloquence in the pulpit. He was kind, gentle, and tender. He lacked the brilliance and aggressive drive that made Grandfather Lanceford B. Wilkes a noted debater, and the ability to fit himself into the company of great leaders of his Christian brotherhood. Nevertheless, Grandfather Pearre was a rare and great man, and well known in his day, and I am proud to have been his grandson.

In the 1890's Dr. Pearre became afflicted with a disease which impaired his ability to walk and, about 1896, he was compelled to retire from the ministry. During his active career, he had been a member of the Masonic fraternity. After retirement, Dr. and Mrs. Pearre lived for a time in Irvington, Indiana, a suburb of Indianapolis. Later they moved to California, Missouri, where they lived with their children. After an illness which lasted several years, Dr. Pearre died January 9, 1904.

The following obituary was published in the *Christian Standard,* January 20, 1904:

Dr. Sterling Elwood Pearre was born in Ohio, August 27, 1825, and departed this life January 9, 1904, in the 80th year of his age. He was a son of Otho Pearre, a descendant of an old Maryland family, and a fellow-worker with Stone, Rogers, and others in the New Light Reformation. S. E. Pearre became a Christian early in life. He graduated from a medical school in 1850, and practiced medicine and surgery with success, until, at the earnest solicitation of friends and a personal sense of duty, he laid down the surgeon's knife and took up the sword of the Spirit, which he wielded with great power in the interests of humanity.

That he might be a more efficient worker for the Master, he entered Bethany College in the beginning of his ministry, from which he graduated with honors in 1855. He was an intimate friend and great admirer of Alexander Campbell, from whose life he drew a wonderful inspiration. He was a profound scholar, a great preacher, and a sedulous worker.

Much of his ministerial work was among our stronger congregations, and many are the "Old Guard" remaining who will remember him with love and veneration for the faithful work he gave the churches in Dubuque, Iowa, Philadelphia, Pennsylvania, Ashland, Ohio, SPRINGFIELD, ILLINOIS, Grand Rapids, Michigan, Indianapolis, Indiana, and other places. He leaves a faithful wife and co-laborer, the organizer of the C. W. B. M. [Mrs. Caroline Neville Pearre], an only daughter, the wife of Elder Wilkes of this city, with their children, a host of friends and a rich heritage of good work for the Master. May his sleep be sweet as he rests from his labors.

S. J. VANCE, Pastor
Christian Church
California, Missouri

✣ ✣ ✣

(1) There is no record as to who Dr. Pearre's first wife was, nor as to the names or number of her children. Their death from yellow fever caused Dr. Pearre to give up the practice of medicine and become a minister.

✣ ✣ ✣

(2) Dr. Pearre's second wife was ANGELINA CARMAN. Letters, still extant, written by her show that in 1851 she was

living in Waynesville, Warren County, Ohio. From her letters, Angelina seems to have been of a sprightly, coquettish nature. Her beautiful handwriting and excellent diction reveal education and culture. An interesting sidelight of her personality is given by her use in 1851 of dainty envelopes for her letters instead of the folded pages, sealed with wax, which were in general use until after the Civil War. The Carman family was talented and musically gifted, with a love for good music.

She and Dr. Pearre had two daughters. The elder daughter was Henrietta (Nettie) Lockwood, born March 5, 1857. She married Edmund Wilkes and became my mother. The younger daughter died of scarlet fever when five years old.

✣ ✣ ✣

(3) The third wife was CAROLINE NEVILLE PEARRE, "Mother of the Christian Woman's Board of Missions." She was born April 15, 1831, near Clarksville, in Montgomery County, Tennessee, and died September 23, 1910.

The portrait shown here is of Dr. Pearre's third wife. Her parents were C. O. Neville and Mary Ross Neville, who moved to Mackinaw, Illinois, when she was quite young. Her mother died when Caroline was fourteen years old.

She spent several years in Walnut Grove Academy, later Eureka College, as a student and as a teacher. She taught sixteen years chiefly in Columbia, Missouri, and in Harrodsburg, Kentucky. She brought to the classroom a fine dignity, tact, and a sparkling sense of humor. While a member of the faculty of Christian College, at Columbia, Missouri, she was one of the teachers of Nettie Pearre. When she married Dr. Pearre, she left the teaching profession, and in middle life assumed the duties of a housewife. As the wife of a minister, Caroline contributed charm, culture, and Christian dedication which matched the ability, scholarship, and fervor of her husband.

Caroline was a woman who exemplified the old-fashioned term "gentlewoman." Possessed of a positive character and eminent qualities of leadership, she exerted a wide influence by her tact and graciousness, without seeming to strive for dominance. She was a person of culture, taste, and discrimination, fastidious in habits of thought, speech, and conduct.

In 1874, while the Pearres were living in Iowa City, Iowa, Caroline's long-standing conviction of the urgent need for vigorous programs of missionary education among women led her to correspond with other women who were prominent in church leadership in various parts of the country. In May, 1874, Mrs. Pearre organized a woman's missionary society in her own church in Iowa City. She wrote to the leading Christian women of other states, urging them to organize missionary societies in their own and neighboring churches. The response was immediate, and several societies were formed. Her letters came to the attention of the brotherhood papers, the *Christian-Evangelist* and *Christian Standard,* and the new movement received their enthusiastic support.

The General Christian Missionary Convention was to meet in Cincinnati, Ohio, in October, 1874. This seemed an opportune time for the women to form a national organization. At the suggestion of Isaac Errett, editor of the *Christian Standard,* about seventy-five women met on October 21 in the basement of the Richmond Street Christian Church in Cincinnati. Mrs. Pearre stated the purpose of the meeting, briefly outlined plans for future work, and moved that a committee be appointed to draft a constitution. She was appointed chairman of that committee. On Thursday morning, October 22, 1874, the constitution of the Christian Woman's Board of Missions was adopted and officials were elected, Mrs. Pearre becoming corresponding secretary. In the afternoon of the same day, the women were invited to report to the General Convention. Mrs. Pearre delivered an address on "Woman's Foreign Mission

Work." The General Convention then passed a resolution recognizing and approving the Christian Woman's Board of Missions.

The full story is told in detail in the *Historical Sketch of the Christian Woman's Board of Missions,* published by the Board at Indianapolis and revised in 1900 by Elmira J. Dickinson; in May, 1905, by Helen E. Moses; and in April, 1911, by Anna R. Atwater (wife of John M. Atwater, pastor of the Springfield church in 1878-1879). In the *World Call* of January, 1948, it is said that she "became known affectionately as the 'Mother of the Christian Woman's Board of Missions.' "

While Mrs. Pearre was living in Indianapolis she contributed articles for young people regularly to the *Young People's Standard,* of which someone said: "Hers is the graceful pen of a ready writer."

First Christian Church of Springfield, Illinois, has reason to take pride in the fact that both the organizer, Mrs. Caroline Neville Pearre, and the last president, Mrs. Anna Robison Atwater, of the Christian Woman's Board of Missions were wives of pastors of this church.

Daniel Radcliffe Howe

Pastor 1862-1864

BORN: 1819, in Ohio
DIED: November 8, 1905, at Eureka, Illinois
MARRIED: Merry ——————
CHILDREN: John Howe
Henry Howe
Merry C. Howe
Elmira Howe
Martha Howe
William F. Howe

Herbert Georg Studio

Daniel Radcliffe Howe

James Howe, the father of the subject of this sketch, was a native of Virginia and a Baptist preacher. He was a member of the Mahoning Association and came with its members into the Restoration movement. So spiritually D. R. Howe was both free-born and of the blood royal. In his youth he attended private schools in Ohio. In 1835 he came with his parents to Bureau County, Ill. There at Leepertown he went to school six weeks to George W. Minier. A little knowledge of Latin and Greek he got by the help of his brother-in-law, Amos Hays. At twenty-one, he taught the first school ever held in Green County, Wis. He became a Christian in his eighteenth year and thereafter preached some for seven years. Then he became a settled minister of the church at Princeton at a salary of $250 a year. He served there through a period of ten years, during the last half of which he received $1,000 per year. He served the churches at Washington two terms, Peoria, *Springfield,* Minonk, Quincy, Putnam, Henry, Lanark two terms, Monroe, Wisconsin two terms; two terms at Princeton, and at Ulysses, Neb. Besides, Mr. Howe was a very successful evangelist and a noted builder of church houses. He was one of the finest men of his time. In him there were combined in an unusual degree the elements of a great gospel preacher. He enlightened the mind by a knowledge of the Scriptures and then appealed to the heart and conscience with great earnestness. Withal, he had fine business ability. During the fifty years of his active ministry he missed the public worship on the Lord's Day only eight times.[1]

He was a charter member of the Princeton Christian Church which was organized March 8, 1840. Later, he was pastor in 1851-1859.

Daniel R. Howe was a member of the House of Representatives, from Bureau County, Illinois, in the Twenty-Third General Assembly, 1862-1864.[2]

And last, but not least, is D. R. Howe, that venerable man of God, who for more than half a century preached with zeal and power Christ, and Him crucified. Thousands of souls rejoiced in salvation and many churches have grown strong by his efforts. He spent some ten of his last years in Eureka, where he served as elder of the Christian Church.

---

[1]N. S. Haynes, *History of the Disciples of Christ in Illinois,* p. 540.
[2]*Blue Book of the State of Illinois,* 1931-1932, p. 758.

This was wise and blessed, for he taught hundreds of young preachers how to grow old sweetly and die gloriously in the faith of Christ.[3]

A letter of August 10, 1961, from Richard Dickinson, of Eureka, Illinois, says:

> Unfortunately, when our church building burned in 1930 our records, up to that time, were lost. Am sorry that I cannot give you any information concerning Mrs. Howe.
>
> I remember Elder Howe quite well as a cheerful and dependable elder who got along agreeably with the younger, and more liberal, members of the Board. Not all elders did, in those days.
>
> In the County Clerk's records I learned that Mr. Howe died November 8, 1905. It is interesting that the attending physician in stating the cause of death, wrote:
>
> > "Old Age. Was not sick, every organ seemed to perform its function. The fruit was ripe and dropt off."

✣ ✣ ✣

The 1860 census records show that Daniel Radcliffe Howe, minister of Disciples of Christ, was living with his wife, Merry, at Princeton, Bureau County, Illinois. Their six children are listed above. This is our only information about MRS. DANIEL RADCLIFFE HOWE.

---

[3]*Obituaries section in Year Book of the Illinois Christian Missionary Society,* 1906; p. 58.

Lanceford Bramblett Wilkes

Pastor 1866-1868

BORN: March 24, 1824, in Maury County, Tennessee

Died: May 1, 1901

MARRIED: Rebecca Kay Bryan, February 7, 1854

CHILDREN: Lucy Boone Wilkes; born October 7, 1854; died December 22, 1857, at the age of 3 years and 2 months.

Mary Ellen Wilkes; born August 29, 1856; died January 24, 1857, at the age of 5 months.

Lewis Bryan Wilkes; born December 8, 1857; died December 4, 1881, at the age of 24 years.

Nannie Dawson Wilkes; born January 30, 1859; died October 17, 1859, at the age of 9 months.

Edmund Wilkes; born November 15, 1860; died December 23, 1943, at the age of 83 years and 1 month.

Anna Huston Wilkes; born May 16, 1862; died July 18, 1862, at the age of 2 months.

John B. Wilkes; born January 14, 1869; died August 24, 1949, at the age of 80 years and 7 months.

Mary Cartmell Wilkes; born April 19, 1870; died July 15, 1870, at the age of 2 months.

Alberta Singleton Wilkes; born July 25, 1871; died February 18, 1893, at the age of 21 years and 7 months.

Herbert Georg Studio

Lanceford Bramblett Wilkes

Herbert Georg Studio

Rebecca Kay Bryan Wilkes

THE WILKES FAMILY

By Edmund Wilkes, Jr.

My grandfather, Lanceford Bramblett Wilkes, minister, educator, author, and religious debater, was the son of Judge Edmund Wilkes and Cynthia Houston Wilkes. When Lanceford was about five years old, his parents moved to what is now Miller County, Missouri.

In 1830 the surrounding region was of distinctly pioneer character. There were then no schools, and post offices and churches were sparsely scattered. Mindful of the need of such community enterprises, Lanceford's father soon organized a school on a corner of his farm and called it Rocky Mount School after the name of the Virginia county seat near where he had been born. It was one of the first if not the first, in the region.

Lanceford early determined to secure a good education; and, by teaching younger pupils and by other work, he earned enough to enter an academy at Springfield, Missouri, where he continued his studies.

Shortly before he entered the academy, he first heard of a religious group newly established in the community. They were known variously as Campbellites, Stoneites, Reformers, Christians, Disciples of Christ, and New Lighters. In later years, Lanceford is quoted as saying that at first he "dispised" them, because their ways were considered uncouth and because of the lack of education of some of those who served as preachers. Lanceford's father is said to have been a Baptist, while his mother was, and remained till her death, a Cumberland Presbyterian. These churches and their members looked upon the "Christian" or "Campbellite" groups as heretical, and opposed them bitterly. However, at Springfield, Missouri, Lanceford came under the preaching of a relative, J. M. Wilkes, who baptized him in the James River near Springfield, Missouri. He decided to become a minister of the Christian Church, and in the spring of 1849 he journeyed to Bethany, Virginia, to enroll in Bethany College under Alexander Campbell. Campbell became his chief mentor and Lanceford became a brilliant disciple and pupil.

At this time, Missouri University came under the leadership of a new president, James Shannon, a native of Ireland, a scholar and a preacher of the Christian Church. In 1850 Lanceford with his younger brother, Peter Singleton Wilkes, became a student at the University of Missouri at Columbia. He completed an extensive course in classical and biblical languages, history, literature, logic, forensics, and attendant subjects. He and his brother received Bachelor of Arts Degrees in 1852, and Master of Arts Degrees in 1855. While a student, Lanceford became an active member of the Union Literary Society.

Meanwhile, in 1851, a school for young women was incorporated. Located at Columbia, Missouri, it was intended as a female counterpart to the University, which restricted its student body to young men. Lanceford B. Wilkes and J. K. Rogers were engaged to travel for the college during the first summer after their graduation from the University. That fall, Wilkes was engaged as vice-principal with W. H. Hopson as principal of the Palmyra Female Seminary, located at Palmyra, Marion County, Missouri. This school had been launched as a feeder school for Christian College. At about the same time, Wilkes became pastor of the Christian Church at Hannibal, Missouri.

In 1856 the first president of Christian College, John Augustus Williams, resigned, and Lanceford B. Wilkes was elected president, with his close friend, Joseph K. Rogers, as his assistant. Wilkes, however, did not enjoy administrative duties and after about two years, in 1856, he resigned as president and was succeeded by Rogers. Wilkes was retained, however, to travel for Christian College.

In 1860 L. B. Wilkes was called again to the pastorate of the Christian Church at Hannibal, Missouri, at which post he continued until 1865. The period of his pastorate at Hannibal was the time of the Civil War. The Wilkes family was unashamedly Southern in its sympathies and inheritance. Because of his Southern views, Wilkes was the object of suspicion on the part of the Northern partisans. He however, confined his activities to the religious field. A story is told that he was arrested, at the instigation of a Union partisan for "preaching the gospel" without subscribing to an oath that he had "never given aid or comfort to the enemies of the United States of America." At the court hearing, Wilkes asked permission to cross-examine the witness who appeared against him. He said to the witness: "You have just testified that you heard me preaching the gospel. Will you please tell the court just what the gospel is?" The witness, in confusion, confessed that he did not know, whereupon the judge pounded his gavel and said: "Case dismissed." Without apology or the least retreat, Wilkes continued a successful pastorate at Hannibal, Missouri.

In November, 1865, Grandfather was called to the pastorate of the Christian Church at Springfield, Illinois, where he stayed for about three years. He came to be recognized among the leaders of the rapidly growing Christian Church, or Disciples of Christ, as the church was becoming known in the Midwest. Since he was widely known for his scholarship, he was often called upon to defend the position of his church in controversies with other denominations. It was an age of religious controversy and acrimony, during which the various denominations battled for influence and supremacy in this pioneer region. Wilkes' reputation grew as the years passed.

About 1868 Grandfather was called to the pastorate of the old Main Street Christian Church in Lexington, Kentucky. This church, located in the Blue Grass region of the state, bore the personal mark of many of the pioneers of the church, such as Alexander Campbell and Barton W. Stone, who in the early 1800's was pastor of the Cane Ridge Church, near Paris, Kentucky. During his pastorate at Lexington, L. B. Wilkes conducted at Mount Sterling, Kentucky, a celebrated debate with Jacob Ditzler of the M. E. Church South, the transcript of which was published in a volume of over 700 pages, and widely circulated among Christian churches of the time.

Some time during 1870, L. B. Wilkes moved to Columbia, Missouri, where he was the pastor of the First Christian Church. During this pastorate, he maintained and enhanced his reputation as a church leader. He was in demand for addresses and conferences, and he contributed many articles to the current religious periodicals. One of his warmest friends was J. H. Garrison, editor of the *Christian-Evangelist.* It was in this period that Grandfather dedicated a new church building, known as Olivet Christian Church, located about six miles east of Columbia, Missouri, on the Fulton Gravel Road. Today Olivet survives as a thriving rural church, a leader in community activities.

Because of health problems in the family, Grandfather moved to Stockton, California, making a place for himself at once. His reputation had preceded him, and he was engaged as pastor of the Christian Church in that city. He continued to write for the church papers, and became the author of a theological book entitled *Moral Evil.*

Grandfather's death occurred on May 1, 1901. The entire group of clergy in Stockton attended his funeral in a body.

Perhaps the best characterization of the work of L. B. Wilkes was made by Dr. W. T. Moore in his book, *The Living Pulpit of the Christian Church* published in 1868 while Grandfather was at Springfield, Illinois. It contains a sermon by Wilkes on "Christ's Precious Invitation." Dr. Moore wrote of his contemporary as follows:

Both as a preacher and teacher, Brother Wilkes has been successful. True, he has never been remarkable for holding "big meetings", and having great success in the evangelical field, though his successes even here have been by no means small; but he has been eminently successful in developing a permanent growth among the Disciples wherever he has labored. He succeeds better as an instructor of the head than as a mover of the heart. And yet he is capable of using very powerful persuasive influence, though he seldom resorts to this method, preferring rather to present his subject in the strongest light to the calm judgment, and await the desired result, which if not as certain, is always more satisfactory when obtained.

His mind is rigidly logical, and yields only to legitimate arguments. He has very strong and decided convictions, and although somewhat reserved in expressing himself on any mooted question, is, nevertheless, always perfectly willing to share the full responsibility of any position he may occupy, and, if necessary, will defend it in the face of all opposition. He is naturally, however, unostentatious, quiet in his general movements, and 'seeks after those things which make for peace.'

He is about six feet high, has light hair, blue eyes, a sallow complexion, and weighs about one hundred and sixty pounds. He is a close, laborious student, and this fact is clearly marked on his physical organization.[1]

✣ ✣ ✣

On February 7, 1854, Lanceford Bramblett Wilkes was married to REBECCA KAY BRYAN, daughter of Lewis Bryan, one of the incorporators and trustees of Christian College at Columbia, Missouri. Lewis Bryan was a leading citizen of Marion County, and was widely known as a breeder of fine horses. He was a generous supporter of higher education for women as well as men.

It will be noted from the list of children born in this family, there were four who did not reach the age of one year. The burdens of child-bearing and of toil, discouragement and bereavement rested most heavily on the mother, Rebecca. She was a person of unusual spirit and character. Her conversation

---

[1] "*The Living Pulpit of the Christian Church,*" by W. T. Moore (Cincinnati: R. W. Carroll & Company, 1868), pp. 145-146.

sparkled with wit and shrewd banter. She could hold her own in any company, and presided graciously over her household. When the family was living in Columbia, Missouri, the young university students would go out to the Wilkes farm home and sit at the bountiful table listening to their hosts, who loved to talk with young men.

Because of much illness in the family and the death of a son, Lewis, Rebecca's health broke and they had to move to California. She never entirely recovered her health, and died January 16, 1888, at the age of 52.

—Edmund Wilkes, Jr.

The portrait of Mrs. Wilkes here shown is from a photograph of an oil painting of her at Christian College, at Columbia, Missouri. Miss Peggy Phillips, Director of Public Relations at that institution, informs us in a letter of January 4, 1961:

> The 60th anniversary of the founding of Christian College, termed the Golden Jubilee, held on May 23, 1911, was the occasion for the hanging of the portraits of the past presidents of Christian College [including Lanceford Bramblett Wilkes] and their wives. The portraits were hung in the new classroom building, Dorsey Hall, which is connected with St. Clair Hall, the administrative building, by a covered loggia. The portraits, richly framed in gold, still hang in the original places designed for them, a main-floor corridor which sees a constant stream of students, faculty, and visitors during each school day. No information as to the artists is available.

Thomas Tilghman Holton

Pastor 1868-1870

BORN: November 17, 1839, near Aberdeen, Ohio
DIED: September 22, 1925, at Lincoln, Illinois
MARRIED: Ellen Margaret Campbell, November 18, 1862
CHILDREN: Helen King Holton (Mrs. C. Lucas)
Campbell Holton; died January, 1959
Pauline Holton
Mary Holton
Anne Carr Holton
Elizabeth Dustin Holton

Herbert Georg Studio

Thomas Tilghman Holton

28118

Herbert Georg Studio

Ellen Margaret Campbell Holton

Thomas T. Holton was born near Aberdeen, Ohio, one of thirteen children of William and Sally Price Tilghman Holton.

He enjoyed superior educational advantages. He went to the country school, to Aberdeen Seminary, to the Southwestern Normal School at Lebanon, O., and graduated from Bethany College July 4, 1862 [as valedictorian]. Before he was seventeen he was a schoolmaster at Genntown, O. On a certificate marked 100 he conducted a school of eighty-five pupils efficiently for nine months. Leaving Bethany after graduation, he served as vice-president of Jefferson College, near Louisville, Ky., of which O. A. Bartholomew was president. Early in 1864, Mr. Holton became the head of Falmouth Academy. Miss Sally E. Holton, his sister, served as assistant. Under their lead this school did superior work for two and a half years. In 1866 he became pastor of the church at Vincennes, Indiana.

. . . In 1868 he became pastor of the church at Springfield, Ill. Next he served the Berlin Church, and at the same time was principal of the public schools there for three years. In 1873 he moved to Lincoln, and served the church there and at Atlanta half-time each.

. . . Later, he served eight years as circuit clerk in Logan County [but continued preaching regularly on Sundays]. Thereafter, . . . he stood for the State Legislature on the Prohibition ticket and received five thousand votes.

. . . When a young man at school, he had for his roommate Ira J. Bloomfield, who won his star in the Civil War. The two attended Sunday school and church together. Being well intentioned, they decided to become members of this church, provided they could be immersed. The minister, however, desired that they should "conform to their religious usage." They were likely lads, so the preacher left with them a booklet entitled "Immersion Not Baptism." This declared that immersion was "unscriptural, inconvenient, and indecent." When the dominie returned he found the lads unchanged. "Well, now," he said, "boys, we want you, and will immerse you if that is your choice." Whereupon, they declared that neither he nor his church had any right to do an unscriptural and indecent thing in the name of the Lord. In 1858, Mr. Holton was baptized by Min. Marsena Stone and received into the Baptist Church. He related no visions nor wonderful experiences. The formula that the preacher used was this: "My brother, upon a confession of your faith in the Lord Jesus Christ and by his authority, I baptize you into the name of the Father and of the Son and of the Holy Spirit, for the remission of sins." Up to this time, this young man had thought to become a lawyer. Now the good Baptist sisters urged him to prepare to preach the gospel. . . . During his four years at Bethany he changed his church affiliation, he entered into the active work of the ministry only by the urgency of the lamented preacher, J. Z. Taylor"[1] [who served this congregation as pastor in 1883-1884].

His first sermon was at Tolesboro, Lewis County, Kentucky, in the summer vacation of 1860. He had gone there to attend a meeting conducted by J. Z. Taylor, the pastor of the Maysville Church. Brother Taylor, without consulting him, announced him for a sermon. He was too abashed to rise up and refuse. To further embarrass him, Brother Taylor left two converts for him to baptize. He borrowed a suit from Brother Halbert and baptized the two men in Cabin Creek in the presence of a large group of people. This was his first experience in baptizing.

While a teacher in Jefferson College, he preached his second sermon at the Cedar Springs Church near Salt River, not very far from Louisville. At the conclusion of the sermon an old farmer came forward, greeted him, and left three dollars in his hand.[2]

During his college career at Bethany he helped to found the Delta Tau Delta college fraternity, which later became a national organization. He was a charter member of its first chapter, and was on the committee that planned and produced the pin worn by the Delts. The intention of the founders was to have a local organization. Therefore, Mr. Holton and several like-minded students visited Washington College at Washington, Pennsylvania, and were initiated into an established college fraternity known as Beta Theta Pi. They then proceeded to organize a chapter at Bethany. Beta Theta Pi had originated in 1839 at Miami University, at Oxford, Ohio.

During 1869 the Illinois Legislature held its regular session in Springfield. The Protestant ministers of the city, including T. T. Holton, took turns in acting as chaplains for both houses, and a fund of $500 was distributed among the ministers for their services. Also, the Constitutional Convention of 1870 was held in Springfield at which each session was opened by prayer. In the record of the proceedings of the convention each prayer

[1]Nathaniel S. Haynes, *History of the Disciples of Christ in Illinois, 1819-1914.* (Cincinnati: The Standard Publishing Company; 1915), pp. 535-537.

[2]A sketch of Thomas Tilghman Holton, covering practically the same matters as above, is found in *History of Logan County, Illinois* (Chicago: Interstate Publishing Company, 1888), pp. 478-479.

is given in full. It shows that on Monday, January 10, 1870, prayer was offered "by the Rev. Mr. Holton," as follows:

O God! Our help in ages past, our hope for years to come. Thou hast watched over us with tender care, and brought us to see the light of this beautiful morning. O Lord! our Heavenly Father, we would not enter upon the labors of this day, without acknowledging Thy guardian care over us—thanking Thee for all Thy goodness and mercy, and praying Thee to take charge of us this day, and guard and keep us as Thou hast in the past. O Lord, Thou hast been our dwelling place in all ages; Thou hast kept us and preserved us. Thou art ever God; Thou openest Thy hand and satisfiest every living creature. All receive their meat from Thee. O God! we would acknowledge Thee in all our ways. We would put our care in Thy hands. We pray Thee to watch us and keep us this day, and while we live, and guide us to Thy honor and glory. O God! forgive us our sins, and bless us more than we can ask of Thee. Give us wisdom and prudence, and enable us to do the great work committed to our hands in such a manner as will gain Thy approbation. Be with the members of this Convention. Give them wisdom, and guide them in their councils. Bless their families from whom they are separated; keep them in peace and quiet. Preserve harmony in these councils. Keep us all in Thy care, and enable us to do that which is good in Thy sight. Keep us all the days of our lives, and when our work is done on earth, bring us down to peaceful graves, and may we so have lived as to be placed on Thy right hand, through our great Redeemer. Amen.

Thirty-second day, Friday, February 4, 1870

The Convention met at ten o'clock A.M., and was called to order by the President.

Prayer was offered by the Rev. Mr. Holton, of Springfield, as follows:

We praise Thee, O Lord; we acknowledge Thee to be our God, and humbly and reverently we would come into Thy presence to adore Thee, the Giver of all good, in whom we live, and move, and have our being.

O God, Thou hast preserved our lives and health through another night, and brought us to the light of this morning under circumstances so favorable to us.

O Lord, we acknowledge Thee in all our ways. We would defer to Thy holy will, and walk in Thy law. O Father, we pray Thee now that Thou wilt forgive us all our sins, and be with us this day. Strengthen us for the work that is before us.

We pray Thy blessing upon this Convention, O God, that it may be guided by the counsels of wisdom, and that great good may follow from the work that is done here during this session. In due time, restore these members, we pray Thee, to their households.

And wilt Thou, O God, be with us, and guide us in all the ways of life. Help us to be true men, and to walk in the ways of truth and love. Go with us, our Father, in all the journey of life. Stand by us in the hour of death; and may we so live that thenceforth we may be with Thee; and to Thy name, O Lord shall be the praise, world without end. Amen.

A copy of the *Lincoln Times* of Thursday, December 15, 1881, is a treasured possession of the Holton descendants. On the first page is a two-column sketch of T. T. Holton under the heading "Pencil Portraits," covering his career up to that date. It mentions as evidence of his personal popularity that in 1876, when Rutherford B. Hayes as Republican candidate for President received a majority of 193 in Logan County, T. T. Holton was elected circuit clerk on the Democratic ticket by 165 votes. He was re-elected in 1880, but continued to preach half time in neighboring churches. He was credited with having done much to systematize the workings of the office of circuit clerk in arranging and indexing papers, copying old and worn-out indexes in order to preserve them, and in bringing up back work. He is described as "a vigorous, persistent toiler."

The following is from an obituary, "He walked with God," in *The Christian-Evangelist,* October 15, 1925, page 32:

The eternal crowning of Elder Thomas Tilghman Holton, took place September 22, 1925. Without a struggle he gently fell asleep and his soul took its flight to that higher and better world. For more than 63 years he preached the gospel of the Son of God. He was active in his chosen work up to Sunday, August 30, at which time he preached his last sermon, at Hallville, Ill., where he had been preaching for half time for more than 25 years. . . .

He was a member of the Second Christian Church of Bloomington, Knights of Pythias and Masonic lodges, Beta Fraternity, McLean County Historical Society and Old Folks Associations.

—David N. Wetzel.

✣ ✣ ✣

The following is contributed by a granddaughter, Mrs. Campbellina L. Odell (Mrs. H. G. Odell), residing at La Jolla, California:

ELLEN MARGARET CAMPBELL HOLTON was born January 9, 1833, in Newry, Ireland, the daughter of Archibald Campbell and Anne Carr Campbell. Archibald was a favorite cousin of Alexander Campbell. When Ellen Margaret was but a few months old, Alexander Campbell arranged for Archibald to come to America with his wife and their family of five.

Ellen Margaret was educated at Pleasant Hill Seminary for girls, which was conducted by Mr. and Mrs. Matthew McKeever, whom she always called "Uncle" and "Auntie Mae." Mrs. McKeever was Jane Campbell, a sister of Alexander.

Nearly all the Campbells conducted schools in Ireland, and they continued doing so in this country.

Ellen Margaret was baptized by Alexander Campbell in Buffalo Creek, back of the church at Bethany. She was a favorite of Alexander Campbell and was in his home a great deal. One evening my grandfather, then a student at Bethany, was an invited guest of Alexander Campbell at dinner—a high honor for an undergraduate. He was seated opposite Ellen Margaret. From that moment he courted her. They were the last couple that Alexander Campbell married.

The marriage occurred November 18, 1862, in the famous old Bethany Church. Alexander Campbell officiated. The attendants were Virginia and Decinia Campbell, daughters of Alexander Campbell; Archie A. Campbell and Jane Campbell, his nephew and niece; Cammie Pendleton, a granddaughter; Miss Emma Blackewell; Miss Sally Holton and Nicholas L. Holton, sister and brother of the groom; Dr. R. F. Turner, W. H. Nave, and Jabez Hall.

Mrs. Holton died April 8, 1922, at Lincoln, Illinois.

James B. Crane

Pastor 1841-1843

BORN: September 22, 1822, at Mentz, Cayuga County, New York

DIED: October 18, 1898, at Waynesboro, Virginia

MARRIED: Charlotte R. ——————

CHILDREN: Son, Daughter } (names not known)

When 14 years of age James B Crane [sometimes spelled Crain] united with the Church of Disciples at Throopsville, in Cayuga county [New York]. Meetings were held there by Alexander Campbell, Dr. Silas E. Shepherd, Erastus Lathrop and Brother Benedict; so that the young man became thoroughly instructed in the great principles which those men advanced and from them received a spirit and inspiration which made him an ardent Disciple until his death.

In 1842 he moved to Paw Paw, Mich., where there were a number of other members from the Throopsville Church, and united with the little congregation which they had organized.

A few years later he and his wife, Mrs. Charlotte R. Crane, went to attend the Western Reserve Eclectic Institute [later Hiram College]. From there they went to Kentucky and took charge of the Kentucky Female College and Highland Institute. He served for some years as superintendent of Mount Pleasant Seminary in Kentucky.

In 1860 they returned to Paw Paw, and for two years had charge of the Union School in that place, where the writer first made their acquaintance and attended their school.

As a teacher he was thorough and genial, and possessed remarkable powers for arousing the noblest ambitions in his students, and winning their highest admiration and love. He gave freely of his out-of-school time to consult and advise with them in regard to their future lives and how to acquire the success for which they hoped. While he was teaching there he was a helper in a protracted meeting held by Brother Wilcox, who was then pastor of the church. Many of the students and others of the young people in the town were converts at the meeting and a fine church was built.

The Professor was full of reminiscences and history of many of those men whom he had personally met, and it was an abiding pleasure to sit at his feet and listen.

In 1860 two rising men had impressed the professor very deeply; they were Isaac Errett, then residing at Ionia, Mich., and James A. Garfield, then president of Eclectic Institute, afterward Hiram College. And during that fall the professor said to the writer: "Garfield has made up his mind to be President of the United States." He lived to see James A. Garfield make his name immortal and honor the death of a President with the exalted and undying glory of a great Christian spirit.

After the close of the school the Professor spent several years in preaching, at which he made a fine success. He had an easy and pleasing delivery and was scholarly, strong, impressive and fearless in declaring the truth.

For several years before his death he had been practicing medicine, both allopathic and homeopathic, and was a skillful physician.

—J. E. Barnum,[1] Denver, Colorado

In the *Millennial Harbinger* of 1868, page 57, is a letter from Crane:

Washington, Pa., Dec. 14th, 1867.

Bro. Pendleton:—I closed a meeting on Pigeon Creek in November, with 31 additions; since which I have been laboring at home. I have just closed a meeting here, with some 50 additions. This is considered a great triumph for the truth in this city. I am now assisting in a meeting at the Valley—the gospel is still triumphing. To God be all the praise. We have among our converts one young man whose mind the Lord has turned toward the ministry. I trust he will honor Bethany ere long, to better qualify himself to plead the Lord's cause.

Fraternally yours,

J. B. CRANE

The following is from the *Christian Standard,* December 17, 1898, page 1660:

The last years of his life he spent in quiet and retirement preparing several books for publication, into which he has gathered the cream of his learning. His wife, with whom he has spent more than 50 happy years, mourns a great loss. A daughter and son, whose affection cheered him, abide on this side while he has crossed over. A grandson, upon whom his heart centered, in young manhood remains to follow him as he followed Christ. The church has sustained a great loss in the death of this soldier of the cross.

A. A. COCKE, D.D., Waynesboro, Virginia

Two of his published books are *Rector W. F. Brand's Pamphlet Reviewed,* and *The Scripture Teacher and practical question book embracing an analysis of the five historical books of the New Testament, designed for Sunday Schools, Bible Classes, families, and private learners.* Both books were published in 1860 and copies of them are in the library of the Disciples of Christ Historical Society at Nashville, Tennessee.

---

[1]J. E. Barnum, "The Professor Sleeps," *The Christian-Evangelist,* Jan. 5, 1899, p. 17.

✣ ✣ ✣

MRS. CHARLOTTE R. CRANE attended Western Reserve Eclectic Institute with her husband, from which both graduated in 1853. The following school year both taught in the English Department of the Institute. James A. Garfield was then a student.

Harvey William Everest

Pastor 1873-1874

BORN: May 10, 1831, at North Hudson, New York
DIED: May 21, 1900, at Des Moines, Iowa
MARRIED: (1) Sarah Ann Harrison, November 4, 1857; died October 20, 1872
Children: Claude Harrison Everest,
Jean Harrison Everest,
Herbert Harrison Everest
(2) Mrs. Jennie Rogers, 1895
Children: None

Herbert Georg Studio

Harvey William Everest

Herbert Georg Studio

Sarah Ann Harrison Everest

Harvey W. Everest[1]

In the short history of the Bible Department of Drake University, three of its five deans have ceased from their labors. A. I. Hobbs and R. T. Mathews have been followed by H. W. Everest. Conspicuous alike for ability, fidelity to all educational interests, and prominent in the affairs of the brotherhood, these men differed widely in characteristics. Doubtless the teacher by instinct, and the more versatile writer among them, was Dean Everest.

He was the well-equipped, all-around educator. He rode no hobbies. His wide range of information, his studious habits and careful mental discipline prepared him admirably for thorough, conscientious treatment of any subject. He was an instructor, not a debater; and his place was in the classroom and councils of his brethren, not in the fray. He was the friend of every enterprise having for its aim and promise the enlightenment and Christianization of the people. The cause of education, with him, ranked next to Christianity.

Harvey W. Everest, A.M., LL.D., was a native of New York, born at North Hudson, May 10, 1831. His parents were of that sturdy, intellectual New England stock which gave a reproduction of these qualities in their son. He attended the public school of North Hudson, and began his career as an educator by teaching a summer school in his own neighborhood when but sixteen years of age. The removal of his parents to the now famous Western Reserve of Ohio gave him the educational advantages offered in the following schools, which he attended in order: Geauga Seminary, Western Reserve Eclectic Institute (now Hiram College), Bethany and Oberlin Colleges—all Ohio institutions except Bethany in West Virginia. At Hiram he was a roommate of James A. Garfield. The two boys worked their way by building houses during the holidays. Upon his graduation from Oberlin, he returned to Hiram as its head instructor—the successor of James A. Garfield, his former associate and friend.

In 1864 he accepted the presidency of Eureka College, and served until called to the pastorate of the Church of Christ at Springfield, Illinois, eight years later.

A professorship was offered him in Kentucky University in 1872, which was taken and filled two years. He returned to Illinois—one year as pastor of the church at Normal, and then as president of Eureka College for the second time. This institution owes to Dean Everest its life and breadth of influence. To him, more than to any other man, is due the uniting of the factions created at old Abingdon. Through

[1]From *The Christian Standard,* June 9, 1900.

these periods, while he was president, young men and women were trained, many of whom have attained eminence as Christian workers.

Butler University, at Indianapolis, Indiana, was opened to him in the spring of 1881, which he entered and served as its president until 1886. In that year a land syndicate organized Garfield University at Wichita, Kansas, and Dean Everest was chosen its chancellor. He was instrumental in raising the $100,000 endowment, provided an excellent curriculum, and met the conditions upon which the university was to become the property of the brotherhood; but the syndicate failed in its financial obligations, never completing the building and removing incumbrances so that it could become the property of the brotherhood. Through no failure of his, the university closed its doors in 1889, and its chancellor became the pastor of the church at Hutchinson. A great sorrow came into his life, in the loss of his devoted and accomplished wife [Sarah A. Everest], while ministering to that congregation.

In 1891 he was made president of the Southern Illinois Normal School at Carbondale. Four years of hard labor, both as instructor and lecturer in that institution, told on his health, and the physical decline began which ended in his death. He was married the second time to Mrs. Jennie Rogers of El Paso, Ill., a woman of refined culture and a noble companion for this great man. He was secured, for the last place in which he served, as dean of the Bible Department of Drake University, in 1897. . . .

In reviewing his whole life, there can be found no reproach upon his character; no just criticism of his spirituality, scholarly attainments and wonderful faithfulness. A keen intellectual discernment, logical, concise, yet considerate of the feelings of those who differed from him, won and held friends for him throughout his whole life. He made large contributions, in his educational work, pulpit and writings, to the plea for the union of God's people in Christ upon the one foundation.

As an author, his "Divine Demonstration" is a textbook on Christian evidences in our colleges. The two more recent works, "Science and Pedagogy of Ethics" and "The New Education" rank high as literary and philosophical productions. His articles on various phases of Christian doctrine in our religious weeklies and periodicals have ever commanded the closest attention and warmest admiration from all classes of readers. He was clear in his thinking, simple and apt in illustration, and, withal, there was a breeze of freshness in the manner in which he presented his thoughts that lent a charm to all he wrote. As a lecturer, he was confined to religious and educational themes, but was sought for addresses from Mississippi to Michigan, and from Pennsylvania to Colorado. As a preacher, he was didactic, not oratorical; but there was no lack of power to hold in closest attention his audience. . . .

So sleeps one of our best-known writers, thinkers, educators.

—I. N. McCASH
University Place Church of Christ, Des Moines, Iowa.

✣ ✣ ✣

(1) Harvey William Everest first married SARAH ANN HARRISON on November 4, 1857. Her portrait is shown here. The chief events in her life are given in a small book entitled *In Memory of Mrs. Sarah A. Everest,*[1] which was privately printed by Mr. Everest. It consists of about fifty unnumbered pages. It contains a tender tribute to her, in prose and poetry, by Mr. Everest, followed by expressions of sympathy from numerous friends, and concludes with selections from her poems and addresses.

The main facts in her life can be briefly set down: Mrs. Sarah Ann Everest was born September 30, 1833, at Painesville, Ohio, and died at Hutchinson, Kansas, 1892, October 20, at 10:20 P.M., having entered upon her sixtieth year. She was of English parentage. William Harrison and his wife (nee Head) came to America from Margate, England, in 1832 and settled on a farm near Painesville, where they lived till near the close of their lives. Sarah was the fourth of their seven children and the eldest daughter. She was a sunbeam in the pioneer's home, a joy to them during all their years, and a ministering angel who tenderly closed their eyes in death. She was educated in the public schools, at Kirtland Seminary, and at the Eclectic Institute, now Hiram College, Ohio, being at times a member of James A. Garfield's classes and of my own. . . . She taught in the public schools with ever increasing success, and at the age of twenty-four became my wife, Nov. 4, 1857, Rev. E. H. Hawley officiating. I was at the time a teacher at Hiram. We lived at Hiram six years, from '57 to '64, during which time I graduated at Oberlin College; at Eureka College, thirteen years, '64-'72 and '77-'81; at Springfield, Ill., two years,

[1]This book does not show name of printer, or date of publication. A copy is now in the possession of their granddaughter, Mrs. Grace Everest McDade Lane, Chattanooga 5, Tennessee, who loaned it to us with permission to quote.

'72-'74; at Kentucky University, Lexington, two years, '74-'76; at Normal, Ill., one year, '76 and '77; at Butler University, Indiana, five and a half years, '81-'86; at Garfield University, Kansas, four years, '86-'90; and at Hutchinson, Kansas, two years, '90-'92. In the cemetery of the latter place now rests her poor body, where neither sun nor storm can disturb its deep repose, but her pure spirit, we believe, has gone to dwell in the house not made with hands, eternal in the heavens. It cannot be that a soul made in the image of God, so responsive to all pure and noble thought, and so filled with love for God and man, has wholly perished. Does Nature preserve her clods but destroy her jewels?

A pen picture of her personal appearance may endure long after every trace has been obliterated from photographs and portraits. She was of medium height and weight; straight and well developed; complexion, a softened brunette; hair, dark brown, at length, sprinkled with gray; eyes, hazel and set in deep, ample orbits; forehead, wide and intellectual; temples, full and distinctly veined; lips, thin, mobile, and relieved by a median projection; shoulders low and waist well proportioned; hands, slender, soft and spiritual; her voice, her own, but low and sweet; the head, so poised as to give a gracious mien; her step, elastic and graceful.

And with all, a deportment so self-respecting and so gentle as to win all hearts.

She became a Christian when sixteen years of age and never wavered in her profession; loved her Bible, loved the church and the dear Lord who gave himself for it.

She gave constantly and liberally, according to her ability, for the cause of missions, asking that I should pay into the treasury of the Christian Woman's Board of Missions her usual amount per year for ten years.

She was a most faithful, intelligent and loving mother. Her maternal heart and hand were never too tender to care for her children. They were never given over to the care of another, and were never neglected. In her discipline there was ever more praise than blame. It was a rule with her never to punish a child when either was angry, nor for an accident; nor to do so before other people. . . .

In everything she was my counsellor; in every trial a source of strength; in every sickness a ministering angel; and if I have done anything worthy, she deserved to share the honor. Because she was my wife I am a better man, for time and for eternity.

H. W. Everest

The next fourteen pages of the memorial book are devoted to letters and resolutions of sympathy. Among these is the following from the widow of President James A. Garfield:

In the early days of the old "Eclectic," while the charm and sentiment of those first words in our "Old Bible"—"In the beginning"—still held it in their spell; when the little band gathered there, filled with the enthusiasm of a new enterprise, gave to the new school strongest devotion, and the members stood together in their grand conceit a phalanx against the world, there came into their midst a bright, young girl, with that luminous beauty which radiates joy and happiness—Sarah Harrison. Easily she took place in the foremost rank; was loved by her associates, and held in high regard as one of their faithful workers. Bright, humorous or grave, as occasion warranted, she was in all worthy places a welcome spirit.

—Lucretia R. Garfield.

The women of this church expressed themselves as follows:

The sad news of Sister H. W. Everest's recent death has deeply moved us. To many of us she was personally known, and greatly esteemed for her high order of mental qualities, and kindness of heart. In her departure from Springfield, where she so well filled the place of our pastor's wife, she left behind her none but most pleasant recollections, of her gentle dignity, and amiable character. She is remembered for the purity of her life, and faithfulness in the conscientious discharge of her duty as a Christian.

We desire to convey to Bro. Everest our sympathy in his bereavement, and we offer him that consolation which may come with the assurance that he is not alone in his grief.

We commend him to the special care of the good Father, who knoweth our frame and without whom not a sparrow falls to the ground.

The Woman's Missionary Society,
First Christian Church, Springfield, Ill.

✣ ✣ ✣

(2) In 1895 Mr. Everest married, MRS. JENNIE ROGERS, of El Paso, Illinois, who died in 1912, in Los Angeles, California. She is described as "a woman of refined culture and a noble companion for this great man."

Edward Thomas Williams

Pastor 1875-1877

BORN: October 17, 1854, at Columbus, Ohio
DIED: January 27, 1944, at Berkeley, California
MARRIED: (1) Caroline Dorothy Loos, August 12, 1884. She died in 1892.
Children: Edward Thrasher Williams
Charles Louis Loos Williams
(2) Rose Sickler, January 8, 1894
Children: Alice Sickler Williams
Gladys Louise Williams

Herbert Georg Studio

Edward Thomas Williams

Herbert Georg Studio

Caroline Dorothy Loos Williams

Edward Thomas Williams was the son of William and Diana Louise (Hughes) Williams. He was ordained as a minister of the Disciples of Christ in 1875, and served his first pastorate in First Christian Church in Springfield, Illinois, 1875-1877. After that he served churches at Denver, 1877-1878; Brooklyn, 1878-1881; and Cincinnati, 1881-1887. On October 23, 1884, he was elected a vice-president of the General Christian Convention. Mr. and Mrs. Williams then went to China as missionaries, as described in *They Went to China,* issued by the United Christian Missionary Society, Department of Missionary Education, in 1948:

Mr. and Mrs. Edward Thomas Williams arrived in Nanking in October of 1887, along with Mr. and Mrs. Meigs. They had been appointed to China in December, 1886. Thus to Mrs. Williams belongs the honor of being our first woman appointed to China [by Disciples of Christ].

Mr. Williams, as a graduate from Bethany College, shared first honors with Ely V. Zollars [pastor of First Christian Church, 1885-1888]. He was already in his fourth pastorate when he was called to foreign service. His wife, Carrie Dorothy Loos Williams, was the daughter of the much revered pastor and college professor, Charles Louis Loos. She was born in Cincinnati, Ohio, while her father was pastor of Central Church. It was from that same church where her husband was pastor that she went out with him to China. She was a refined and cultured young woman and a successful teacher. Mr. and Mrs. Williams took their two young sons with them to China. The sons later took up their life work there. The older, Edward Thrasher Williams, in 1943 retired from his post as Commissioner of Customs in Wuchow, Free China. In 1947 the second son, Charles Louis Loos Williams, retired from his post in the United States War Department. . . .

In 1891, Mr. and Mrs. Williams were forced to return to America because of the ill health of Mrs. Williams. She died following an operation.

Mr. Williams returned alone to his work. He had an unusual aptitude for the Chinese language. Besides, he was a true missionary statesman. He took charge of the evangelistic work, had a regular circuit for preaching which included Drum Tower and South Gate in Nanking, Pukow across the river, Hsiakwan on the Yangtze at Nanking and also more distant places.

In 1896, Mr. and Mrs. Williams resigned from the mission and moved to Shanghai to enter into literary and consular work. . . . Mr. Williams' brilliant career included work with the United States government in China and the United States, and with the Chinese government. He continued in the diplomatic service until 1918 when he was appointed Agassiz Professor of Oriental Languages and Literature in the University of California. He held that position until he retired as Professor Emeritus in 1927. Professor Williams lived in retirement at his home in Berkeley until his death on January 27, 1944.

Edward Thomas Williams is one of five pastors of the First Christian Church who were written up in *Who's Who in America.* The other pastors are Ely Vaughn Zollars, Charles Clayton Morrison, Frederick William Burnham, and William Fredric Rothenburger.

In the diplomatic service from 1896 to 1918 he was interpreter in Shanghai; translator in Shanghai; secretary, American Legation, Peking; consul-general, Tientsin; assistant chief, Division of Far Eastern Affairs, Department of State; chief, Division of Far Eastern Affairs, Department of State.

At the time of entering the diplomatic service, Mr. and Mrs. Williams withdrew from the Disciples of Christ and became Unitarians.

After World War I, he was Technical Delegate to the Peace Conference in Paris, 1919.

His foreign decorations include the Chinese Order of the Golden Sheaf in 1918, of which he became an officer in 1919 and the Blue Ribbon Order of Jade in 1936.

He was the author of *Recent Chinese Legislation,* 1904; *The State Religion of China Under the Manchus,* 1913; *China Yesterday and Today,* 1923; and *A Short History of China,* 1928.

A biographical sketch of Mr. Williams appears in 18 biennial issues of *Who's Who in America* from Volume 6, 1910-

1911, to and including Volume 23, 1944-1945; also in *Who Was Who in America,* Volume 2, 1943-1950, page 579.

✣ ✣ ✣

(1) MRS. CAROLINE DOROTHY LOOS WILLIAMS was born February 21, 1856, in Cincinnati, Ohio. She was the daughter of Charles Louis Loos, then pastor of Central Church in Cincinnati, Ohio, and later president of Eureka College and also of Kentucky University, now Transylvania. When she was two years old, the family moved to Bethany, Virginia, where her father had been appointed to the chair of Ancient Languages in Bethany College. As she grew up, she knew Alexander Campbell, Walter Scott, Dr. Robert Richardson, President Pendleton, Isaac Errett, Judge Jeremiah Black (Attorney General), and all the illustrious men who were accustomed to visit Bethany. At the age of 15, under her father's preaching, she united with the church and was baptized by him in Buffalo Creek, near the Bethany campus.

She attended the public schools and "a select school" in Bethany, Virginia; Steubenville Female Seminary; and spent two years in the Normal School at Dayton to prepare herself for teaching. After completing the course, she taught for some time in the schools of that city. The year before her marriage, she taught German and French in Christian College at Columbia, Missouri. She married Edward Thomas Williams on August 12, 1884.

She became the first woman appointed as a missionary in China. At Nanking, they lived for two years in a Buddhist temple. Because of the riots and threatening conditions, the missionary women and children were sent, for safety, to Shanghai. Mr. Williams and the other men remained in Nanking to carry on the work as best they could in the chapels, schools, hospitals, and dispensaries.

In December, 1891, an examination disclosed that Mrs. Williams needed a delicate and difficult surgical operation. The physicians in Nanking and Shanghai were unwilling to perform it. The case was urgent. No time was to be lost if her life was to be saved. In a few days, she and her family were on board ship on their way home. The ship reached port two days before the scheduled time. The day before the operation, she wrote a letter to her two little boys, to be opened in case she did not recover. She died February 12, 1892. Hers was the first death in the China Mission.

Her funeral service was held February 14, 1892, in the Central Christian Church in Cincinnati, Ohio. It was announced: "Other services of a similar character will be held in China, in India, in Japan, in Great Britain, in Lexington, in Columbus, in Dayton, in Bethany, and in other places where her great moral worth and heroic services are known. This service today is only one of many that will be held to honor her."

✣ ✣ ✣

(2) ROSE SICKLER was the first single woman appointed to China. She was a Pennsylvania girl, a graduate from a state normal school, and was sent to China in 1890 to establish educational work for girls. When the school was discontinued, she took up evangelistic work in Nanking. There in 1894 she married Mr. Williams. She shared with him in his itinerations, and besides found time to translate several children's books, and to carry on work among Chinese women.

John Milton Atwater

Pastor 1878-1879

BORN: June 3, 1837, at Mantua, Ohio

DIED: January 17, 1900, at Cleveland, Ohio

MARRIED: (1) Harriet Smith, 1863; died 1887.

Children: Frank Atwater, died in early childhood

Ernest Atwater, missionary in China; killed in Boxer Rebellion, 1900

Fred Atwater, died May, 1901

Mabel Atwater, wife of Dr. C. B. Taylor, of Nassau, Iowa

(2) Anna Robison, June 1892; died March 23, 1941

Children: None

Herbert Georg Studio

John Milton Atwater

Herbert Georg Studio

Anna Robison Atwater

John Milton Atwater . . . was the third child of Darwin and Harriet Clapp Atwater. He entered the Eclectic Institute at Hiram in 1851, and each year for ten years following was connected with the school as student or tutor. He entered Oberlin College in '61, and was graduated from there in '63. . . . After graduation he spent two years in the theological course at Oberlin. Then, returning to Hiram, he became principal of Eclectic Institute during its last year, and upon its becoming Hiram College [in 1867] he was its first professor of Latin and Greek. From '68 to '70 he was president. The following year was spent in Alliance College as professor of Latin and Greek. He had begun preaching in 1859, and had continued it during all his school work. From '71 to '87 he gave himself exclusively to the ministry [he served as pastor of the Christian Church at Springfield, Illinois, 1878-1879] except that in the fall of 1880 he took President B. A. Hinsdale's place at Hiram, while he was engaged in the Garfield campaign. At the opening of Garfield University in 1887, he was made head of its normal department and professor of Didactics. Financial failure closed that school, and he went to Eureka College [as president in 1892-1893]. . . . As he was about to enter upon his second year at Eureka he was called to Oskaloosa College as its president. In '97 he accepted a call to Central Christian College, Missouri. Just as he was on the entrance of that work his health suddenly failed. He never took up regular work again, but did much preaching in various places while seeking to regain his strength. He died January 17, 1900, at Cleveland, Ohio, among the friends of the Franklin Circle Church, where he had been pastor from '79 to '84.[1]

❖ ❖ ❖

(1) In 1863 while they were still in school MISS HARRIET SMITH and John M. Atwater were married. She died in 1887.

❖ ❖ ❖

(2) In June, 1892, Atwater married MISS ANNA ROBISON. She was born on a farm near Cleveland, Ohio, and graduated from Hiram College in 1882. She served several years as principal of the high school at Bryan, Ohio, before her marriage to John M. Atwater. After his death in 1900,

[1]J. M. Atwater, *Jehovah's War Against False Gods,* (St. Louis: Christian Publishing Co., 1903), p. 355.

she resumed teaching, and for three years was president of the Ohio Christian Woman's Board of Missions. In 1904 she was called to National Headquarters, and acted as vice-president of the Christian Woman's Board of Missions, under Mrs. Helen E. Moses as president, from 1904 to 1907. She also edited *Missionary Tidings,* the official magazine.

Mrs. Atwater served as vice-president of the Christian Woman's Board of Missions from 1904 to 1907, when at the death of Mrs. Moses she succeeded her in the presidency. In this significant post of leadership she served from that date until the C. W. B. M. united with other brotherhood agencies to form the United Christian Missionary Society in 1920.

During these years Mrs. Atwater brought to the work a high quality of leadership. She saw the annual receipts of the Board grow from $281,637.54, in 1907 to $691,950.93, in 1919. In the period of her presidency she also saw the assets increase from $300,000 to $1,446,-588.

. . . The Board carried on home missionary work in the great cities, among the Negroes of the South, and among the southern highlanders and elsewhere. It pioneered in establishing Bible Chairs at state universities, the first of these being that at the University of Virginia. Others which followed were at Ann Arbor, Michigan, and Lawrence, Kansas. Even more inclusive was the foreign work of the C. W. B. M., extending to India, South America, Africa and islands of the sea, and including in its work programs of evangelism, education, social reconstruction and medical service. . . .

In all the years of her leadership in the field of missions, Mrs. Atwater was characterized by an indefatigable energy, and intellectual ruggedness and a vast breadth of vision. Her realistic sympathy, her capacity for careful administration and her unusual speaking ability were assets which the brotherhood recognized and prized.[2]

In the same issue of World Call, Dr. Robert M. Hopkins, then president of the United Christian Missionary Society, wrote of her:

Mrs. Anna R. Atwater has been one of the outstanding women of our brotherhood. From 1905 to 1926 she made a vital contribution in kingdom service through the Christian Woman's Board of Missions

---

[2]From "Anna R. Atwater," by George W. Buckner, Jr., in *World Call,* May, 1941, p. 13.

and the United Christian Missionary Society; in both organizations she graced executive positions of trust and responsibility. To her comrades at headquarters, to her associates in state organizations, to the brethren, both brothers and sisters, among the churches, to the missionaries on the fields at home and abroad, she was a constant source of inspiration and encouragement. Her life was one of varied interests and of worthwhile achievements.

Joseph Buford Allen

Pastor 1879-1883

BORN: 1847, in Kentucky
DIED: 1902, at Spokane, Washington
MARRIED: No information

Joseph Buford Allen was the youngest of three brothers who served in the Christian ministry—Dr. J. M. and J. W. Allen being the other two. He was educated in the public schools of Bloomington and at Eureka College. He began the study of law with Judge W. E. Nelson, of Decatur, but soon decided to enter the ministry. Besides other congregations in Illinois, he served the First Church in Springfield for a period of four years. His health failing, he moved to Hutchinson, Kan., and later to Spokane, Wash.

Mr. Allen was a clear and vigorous thinker, a sincere and frank man and an efficient preacher.[1]

Two landmark events occurred during Joseph Buford Allen's pastorate—first, incorporation of the church; and, second, the erection and dedication of a new church building (the third). On March 10, 1880, the church became incorporated as a religious corporation under the name "The Christian Church of Springfield, Illinois." The trustees were Stephen T. Logan (Lincoln's second law partner), Jonathan R. Saunders, William Lavely, Dr. Vachel T. Lindsay (father of Vachel Lindsay, poet), Charles P. Kane and Samuel H. Twyman. The certificate of incorporation was recorded March 15, 1880, in the office of the County Recorder of Sangamon County as doc. 21008, vol. 80M, page 9.

On February 29, 1880, a committee consisting of A. H. Saunders, H. C. Latham and the deacons of the church was appointed to negotiate the sale of the church property at Sixth and Jefferson streets.

The new building was dedicated February 12, 1882, in a union service in which many ministers of other Springfield churches participated. The dedicatory sermon was preached by Andrew Jackson Kane, who had been pastor in 1847-1851. In conclusion Elder Allen said: "Thus do we throw open our doors. Thus do we dedicate this house to the service and to the true worship of God."

[1]Nathaniel S. Haynes, *History of the Disciples of Christ in Illinois, 1819-1914.* (Cincinnati: The Standard Publishing Company, c 1915.)

On Monday, February 13, 1882, the daily *Illinois State Journal* contained an account of the dedicatory program, covering three full columns, and said editorially:

> The new Christian Church, which was dedicated yesterday, is really the best designed and the neatest temple of worship in this city. It is sufficiently roomy to meet all the ordinary wants of the congregation, and yet not so large as to cause a moderate-sized audience to be lost or feel lonely. There is such an air of taste and comfort about all the finishing and furnishing as to make it a most agreeable Sabbath-day home. It is a credit to our city, and doubly a credit to the good judgment, liberality and Christian benevolence of the congregation who built it. There are other religious societies in the city that ought to be inspired by, and imitate, this example.[2]

---

[2]A picture of this church building is on page 18.

John Z. Taylor

Pastor 1883-1884

BORN: November 6, 1830, near Bakersville, Pennsylvania
DIED: October 28, 1889, in Kansas.
MARRIED: Mary Stuart
CHILDREN: Clara, youngest
Names or number of other children, not known

John Z. Taylor was considered by many to be the greatest evangelist of his day. His success is evidenced by published letters referring to the large number of additions resulting from his evangelistic meetings in various places. As an example, in the *Millennial Harbinger* of 1866, a letter from O. A. Burgess says:

> Indianapolis, April 10, 1866: Dear Bro. Pendleton:—About the tenth of Feb. our preachers resident here commenced a meeting and continued it thirty-two days. They were assisted ten days by Bro. J. Z. Taylor, whom you will remember as a graduate of Bethany College—and one that reflects honor upon his Alma Mater, being a workman that needeth not to be ashamed. The immediate results of the meeting were one hundred and twenty additions to the church.

From 1873 to 1875, before coming to this church, J. Z. Taylor had been pastor of the First Christian Church at Springfield, Missouri, which changed its location to Campbell and College Streets and celebrated its forty-first anniversary. At that time it was reported that his Sunday night audiences would number 700, in a city of 9,000 people. From 1875 to 1881 he was pastor of the First Christian Church at Kansas City, Missouri.

The following excerpts are from "Illinois Notes" in *The Christian-Evangelist:*

> Springfield, April 2 [1883]—The church at Springfield is alive and doing a fine work. J. Z. Taylor, of Kansas City, is now holding a meeting of some days. The Sisters are anxious to push the work to higher heights of usefulness and have already accomplished a glorious work. Sister Cora Logan's name glides fragrant amid the purest memories of the church as the enthusiastic agent of *The Christian-Evangelist,* and Dr. Lindsay and his talented helpmeet labor on, ever fondly and devotedly for the mighty cause. God bless the church at Springfield.
>
> —Gay

Elder Taylor himself comments:

Springfield, April 16.—We have a fine meeting in progress here. Have had 24 additions; 21 confessions to date. The Dr. Munhall meeting is to close to-night, which will, I think, open a wider field for our work.

J. Z. Taylor

Springfield, May 1.—Bro. J. Z. Taylor, of Kansas City has been with us a month. Last night he closed the most successful protracted meeting we have had in this place in years. Forty-four were added to the church, forty of them by confession. Calmness and deliberation characterized the meeting, and the additions are of good material. The church is greatly built up and encouraged. Bro. Taylor is a man of musical abilities, as the people of Missouri must already know. With untiring zeal he has wielded the power of his cultured mind and consecrated heart for the advancement of the cause here, and he will long be gratefully remembered by the church in Springfield.

V. T. Lindsay

In "Our Budget" of *The Christian-Evangelist* of April 19, 1883, appears the following:

Bro. J. Z. Taylor will go to Montana Ter. as the missionary of the Woman's Board, in June. He is a splendid man for the field, and we congratulate the sisters on the wisdom of their choice. All Disciples will rejoice that they have sent so good a man to so important a field. We shall expect to hear of a great work accomplished.

To which Mr. Taylor replied:

The following explains itself: In your "budget" you alluded to the fact that I am going to Montana to labor in the interest of the Christian Woman's Board of Missions. This is true. But I am going for a limited time only. In response to the urgent appeal of those earnest women I have consented to go and inaugurate the work. I write this that my limited stay may not be misunderstood.

J. Z. Taylor.

In the August 2, 1883, issue of *The Christian-Evangelist,* "Personal Mention" is made as follows: "J. Z. Taylor has accepted a call to labor at Springfield, Ill., and will enter upon his work on his return from Montana."

As a writer, J. Z. Taylor appears as the author of a treatise in the same book with Alexander Campbell, in a volume entitled *A Symposium of the Holy Spirit.* It was published by John Burns at St. Louis, Missouri, in 1879, containing the following chapters:

Consciousness and Its Relation to the Holy Spirit, by A. B. Jones;
The Holy Spirit in Consciousness, by G. W. Longan;
The Holy Spirit in Consciousness, by Thomas Munnell;
The Witness of the Holy Spirit, by J. Z. Taylor;
The Influence of the Holy Spirit on Conversion and Sanctification, by Alexander Campbell.

The authors, with the exception of Campbell, were Midwest preachers living in Missouri and Illinois.

J. Z. Taylor was one of the Illinois delegates to the General Christian Missionary Convention in St. Louis on October 20, 1884.

After leaving Springfield, J. Z. Taylor resumed his career as an evangelist. The *Christian Oracle* of May 7, 1885, quotes from the *Chicago Tribune:*

> The Rev. J. Z. Taylor, of Kansas City, has been conducting revival services during the last week at the Central Christian Church at the corner of Indiana Avenue and Twenty-fifth Street [Chicago]. Mr. Taylor has had large success as an evangelist, and is a speaker of unusual power. He was greeted yesterday morning with the largest audience assembled in the church for years.

An obituary of J. Z. Taylor in *The Christian-Evangelist* of December 26, 1889, written by J. W. Newland, a former parishioner at Bedford, Indiana, says that Taylor began his pastorate in that city the first of April, 1868.

> While he was our pastor, the church in Bedford enjoyed the high noon of its prosperity and influence. All his sermons had in them a purpose; there was nothing perfunctory about them. He was not exegetical or explanatory. His texts were suggestive merely of the line of thought he designed to pursue. His discourses were always logical.

He first laid down his premises, slowly, coolly, dispassionately. These were always made as plain as possible, so as to be within the comprehension of all. Then from these premises he drew his conclusions. This part of his sermon was presented with great power and indescribable earnestness. Then followed an exhortation to the church, appealing to the membership to have more zeal and earnestness for the salvation of sinners, and lastly, an appeal to sinners, full of pathos and tenderness, to turn away from sin and lay hold of the hope set before them in the gospel. His manner in the pulpit was exceedingly earnest and impressive. His whole soul was full of the thought that he had a message to the world. The whole man, body, soul and spirit, was engaged while he was preaching. His sermons were always fresh. . . .

Finally I would say of his preaching, that its effects in communities where he labored were profound and lasting. His logic and sound reasoning convinced the understanding, his earnestness and touching pathos moved the people to obedience, and while thousands have come into the church under his preaching, they not only CAME, but they knew WHY they came.

✣ ✣ ✣

MISS MARY STUART was living at Somerset, Pennsylvania, when she met and married J. Z. Taylor. Mrs. Taylor was a life member of the C. W. B. M., and the youngest daughter, Clara, was the assistant secretary. We have no information as to the number or names of the other children.

Ely Vaughn Zollars

Pastor 1885-1888

BORN: September 19, 1847, at Lower Salem, Ohio
DIED: February 10, 1916, at Warren, Ohio
MARRIED: Hulda Louisa McAtee, October 22, 1865
DAUGHTER: Addie Zollars (Mrs. Harlan Page)

Herbert Georg Studio

Ely Vaughn Zollars

Herbert Georg Studio

Hulda Louise McAtee Zollars

By Ronald E. Osborn

Ely Vaughn Zollars was a distinguished minister and educator among the Disciples of Christ, who first came to prominence with his call to the pastorate of First Christian Church in Springfield, Illinois, in 1885. He was born near Lower Salem, about thirteen miles from Marietta, Ohio, on September 19, 1847. His boyhood was that of a village blacksmith's son. After his marriage to Hulda Louisa McAtee in October, 1865, he engaged briefly and unsuccessfully in the mercantile business, then took up farming and taught country school on the side. In 1871 he entered Bethany College to study for the ministry. He earned his B.A. in 1875, sharing the first honors of the class with Edward T. Williams, who also became pastor of First Christian Church in Springfield, 1876-1878, and who later was a missionary in China. In 1876 Zollars received his M.A. degree from Bethany. In 1894 Hiram College conferred on him the degree of LL.D. He was ordained to the ministry at the Bethany Church in 1876, and served the college briefly as adjunct professor of ancient languages and as financial agent. From 1877 to 1884 he was president of Kentucky Classical and Business College at North Middletown, Kentucky, and for one year (1884-1885) he presided over Garrard Female College at Lancaster, Kentucky.

When Zollars came to Springfield, Illinois, in 1885, First Christian Church had about three hundred members and paid its minister an annual salary of $1800. He began on the third Sunday in June, with a sermon on "Duties of Pastor and People." His pastorate was a time of hard work and vigorous growth. He put the membership to work on committees, organized a program of calling on absentees, and founded a Sunday evening youth group (young people's prayer meeting) which soon had a regular attendance of about forty. In December he held a two-week meeting, and in February he began a protracted meeting with services every night except Saturday for ten weeks; except at five services, Zollars did all the preaching. At the end of his first year, he reported 221 additions. During the next two years, he was in increasing demand as a speaker throughout Illinois and adjoining states; nevertheless, in his three-year pastorate the membership doubled to more than six hundred.

In the second year of Zollars' ministry, a parsonage was erected on a lot back of the church building. Here Mrs. Zollars, who seemed retiring in public, made her influence felt. Their daughter, Addie, was nineteen when the family came to Springfield; she was a talented musician and gave her father considerable help. The Zollarses were particularly close friends of the [Dr. Vachel T.] Lindsays; in the scarlet fever epidemic of 1888, three of the Lindsay children died, and Zollars conducted the funerals. Later, because of the closeness of the families, Vachel and Olive (Wakefield) Lindsay were sent to Hiram College.

During Zollars' ministry, the organ began to be used in the Sunday worship of the church. He preached vigorous sermons on the position of Disciples, on home and foreign missions, on temperance, and on American destiny. He welcomed to the pulpit ministers of Methodist, Presbyterian, and Lutheran churches. At the request of the ministers of the city, he met in debate on the Sabbath question with the famous D. M. Canright; not long afterward, Canright abandoned the Seventh-Day Adventists. In August, 1887, when the great railroad disaster occurred at Chatsworth, Illinois, Zollars was waiting for a train at a nearby station and saw the rescue operations, as well as the scene of the wreck; back in Springfield on a Sunday evening he delivered an eloquent sermon on "The Chatsworth Horror."

Eureka College sought Zollars for its president, but without success. Twice he turned down the presidency of Hiram; the trustees of the latter school persisted, however, and in June, 1888, he was inaugurated to his new post. In an administration of fourteen years, Zollars brought Hiram College to larger fame and usefulness than it had ever enjoyed, emphasizing particularly the education of the ministry. From 1902 to 1906 he was president of Texas Christian University at Fort Worth, Texas. Then he undertook the founding of Oklahoma Christian University (now Phillips University) at Enid, Oklahoma, which he served as president until the time of his death. He was the author of eight books, the best known being *The Great Salvation* (1895) and *The Commission Executed* (1912).

While Zollars preached throughout his long career, the church at Springfield, Illinois, was his only full-time pastorate. On the second anniversary of their coming, the congregation honored Elder and Mrs. Zollars with a reception. She was given a gold-headed umbrella and he a gold-headed cane. Fifty years later, Mrs. Addie Zollars Page, their only child, presented the cane once more to the church, which in turn entrusted it to the Disciples of Christ Historical Society at Nashville, Tennessee.

Edward Anderson, a young man during Zollars' Springfield ministry and a long-time superintendent of the Sunday school of First Christian Church, wrote in 1939: "Among all these distinguished ministers, I think I am safe in saying that Brother Zollars was one of the most God-fearing, God-loving, Christ-like men we ever had."

After only a few weeks at Hiram College, the new president expressed himself in the *Christian Oracle* of September 27, 1888, as follows:

Hiram College opened on August 23, 1888, under auspicious circumstances. There is an increase in the number of students over last year of fully 23 per cent, and the school last year increased 15 per cent over the previous year. One very encouraging feature is the large number of ministerial students in attendance. Owing to the phenomenal attendance in the ministerial department a movement is being inaugurated to endow the Bible chair this year, and already two or three quite handsome subscriptions have been made. Another cheering feature of the school is the fact that the patronage seems to be extending over a continually growing field. Some eleven or twelve states besides Canada are represented this year.

Faculty, students and citizens of Hiram are all very elated over the present outlook. September 18, 1888, E. V. Zollars

A biographical sketch of President Zollars appears in *Who's Who in America,* in 12 biennial volumes, from Volume 1, 1899-1900, to and including Volume 12, 1922-1923; also in *Who Was Who in America,* Volume 1, 1897-1942.

✣ ✣ ✣

MRS. HULDA LOUISA McATEE ZOLLARS was born September 6, 1846, in Iowa, and died in August, 1925, at Hiram, Ohio. She was the daughter of Dudley McAtee, a doctor during the Civil War, and she assisted him in caring for the soldier boys who were ill. She and Mr. Zollars were married at an early age—she at 19 and he at 18. They first lived on a farm where their only child, Addie, was born. They then moved to Bethany, Virginia, while Mr. Zollars was attending Bethany College. Wherever they lived, Mrs. Zollars took a special responsibility for looking after the home life of the young women. When they retired, they went back to Hiram for the balance of their lives.

John Benton Briney

Pastor 1888-1891

BORN: February 11, 1839, at Botland, Nelson County, Kentucky.

DIED: July 20, 1927, at Rural Retreat, Virginia

MARRIED: Lucinda Holbert

CHILDREN: William Newton Briney
Russell Benton Briney
Campbell Briney
John Benton Briney, Jr.
Jessie Briney (Mrs. J. Basil Keesling)
Annie Briney (Mrs. W. H. Kelly)
Willie Briney (daughter)

Herbert Georg Studio

John Benton Briney

Herbert Georg Studio

Lucinda Holbert Briney

John Benton Briney . . . was brought up to farm work, receiving such education as could be obtained in the country schools of those days, in an attendance of two or three terms. At the age of sixteen years he apprenticed himself to learn the carpenter's trade, serving a term of three years as an apprentice. For this service he received thirty dollars the first year, forty dollars the second, and fifty dollars the third. He worked at his trade three years after the expiration of his apprenticeship, and then married and spent a year at farming. In the meantime he began to try to preach a little in connection with his other employments, and receiving some encouragement from various brethren, he determined to devote his life to the ministry of the Word of God.

Having formed such a purpose, and seeing the importance of a good education on the part of a minister, he entered Eminence College, at Eminence, Kentucky, whose president was W. S. Giltner, who conducted the college with marked ability and success for many years. In this institution Mr. Briney took a four years' course, one year before the close of which he was called to minister to the large church in Eminence—a distinction of which a young man might be proud. After serving that church three years he went to Millersburg, Kentucky, and preached for the church there and the one at Carlisle two years. He then went to Winchester, Kentucky, for four years, and then to Maysville, same state, and after preaching there four years, he became state evangelist for Kentucky. After serving in that capacity two years, he again took up the work in Maysville, not having removed his family from that place.

After another term of two years in Maysville, he went to Covington, Kentucky, where he preached for two years and a half, and then, for a change, he evangelized about six months—mostly in the state of New York. Following this he spent a few months in Maysfield, Kentucky, preaching for the church there, and organizing West Kentucky College. In 1886 he was called to the Linden Street church, Memphis, Tennessee, and after laboring there two years and a half he went to Springfield, Illinois, where he ministered to the church thirty months, and then accepted a call to Tacoma, Washington. It was while preparing to go to Tacoma, that he met with the accident that resulted in an intercapsular fracture of the hip which lamed him for life, and kept him confined to the house for nearly a year, and on crutches for about two years. It was during this confinement that he wrote *The Form of Baptism,*[1] and *The Temptations of Christ.*

[1]Although *The Form of Baptism* was not an oral debate, it belongs in the class of public controversies between ministers of the Disciples of Christ and those of other denominations. This one is notable in being probably among the last of such controversies to be printed. We noted supra that Jeremiah P. Lancaster, pastor 1843-1844, participated in one of the first of such debates to be printed.

His first work in the ministry after his injury was in Knoxville, Tennessee, where he labored one year and then went to Moberly, Mo., where he did the heaviest work of his life in the ministry. After serving the Moberly church nearly seven years he spent a year in the evangelistic field, and started *Briney's Monthly,* which was a success from the first issue, and after running through four volumes, lacking one number, it now merges into the *Christian Companion.* . . . During Mr. Briney's long and arduous ministerial life he has held about thirty discussions with representatives of the leading religious bodies of this country, besides lecturing considerably on scientific and other subjects.[2]

The Form of Baptism, referred to above, attracted nationwide attention at the time. It was written in Springfield during Mr. Briney's convalescence from his hip injury, and was published serially in *The Christian-Evangelist.* Later it was issued in book form. The subtitle reads:

An Argument Designed to Prove Conclusively that Immersion Is the Only Baptism Authorized by the Bible.

It is a scholarly 188-page treatise, quoting exhaustively from Greek literature in the original, supported by recognized lexicographers. Then follows a 52-page answer by Joseph L. Tucker, D. D., rector of Christ Church, Mobile. Mr. Briney closes with a "Reply to Dr. Tucker's Review," which covers 49 pages.

According to the preface:

This book grew out of novel and interesting circumstances. In 1891 Dr. R. P. Huger, Episcopalian, and Dr. E. C. Anderson, Disciple, both of Anniston, Ala., had some friendly conversations as to the scriptural form of baptism, and the former submitted to the latter the following proposition:

"I hereby offer one thousand dollars ($1,000) for conclusive evidence that immersion is taught as Christian baptism—that is, as the only form of Christian baptism taught by the Bible. The judges shall be composed of five clergymen of the Protestant Episcopal Church, to be chosen by me, and five men to be chosen by Dr. E. C. Anderson.

R. P. Huger"

[2]Brown, John T., *Churches of Christ* (Louisville: John P. Morton and Co., 1904), p. 470.

Ten judges were selected, five by each side. An effort was made by Dr. Anderson to have an odd number, but this was rejected. The result was a divided verdict, five to five. The $1,000 was never paid.

Dr. Homer Wilson Carpenter, now retired and living at Louisville, Kentucky, relates the following in a letter of February 11, 1961:

> Those of us who knew J. B. Briney will recall him as a great debater. In our National Conventions he was frequently a dramatic figure.
>
> In the Pittsburgh Convention in 1909, the Convention Committee brought in a recommendation to go, the next year, to Norfolk, Virginia. It was rather taken for granted that this action would be taken. Then, to the surprise of the committee, J. B. Briney slowly came to the front of the platform. Wichita, Kansas, had made a strong fight for the next convention, but had failed with the committee.
>
> As Briney began to speak, in the midst of the platform and directly behind him, there was raised a great sun flower. Its height was from the floor to the top of the open platform. Under a spotlight its golden glow filled the whole platform. The audience was electrified by the dramatic surprise. And when Briney had finished his speech in favor of Wichita, a substitute motion turned the next convention from Norfolk to Wichita.
>
> The above incident was rather characteristic of the man, who in his generation was one of our giant leaders in the Christian Church.

From the obituary in *The Christian-Evangelist* of August 4, 1927:

> J. B. Briney
>
> *Faces the rising sun as he passes into the Great Beyond after a life marked by stalwart battling for the Cross.*
>
> J. B. Briney, honored prince of the King, went on at the rising of the sun, July 20, 1927. He was born at Botland, Nelson County, Ky., Feb. 11, 1839. He attained the advanced age of 88 years.
>
> When the end came, Brother Briney was at the home of his devoted daughter, Mrs. J. B. Keesling, Rural Retreat, Va. For several years he had spent his summers in this kindly home. Protracted cold this season brought on pneumonia. . . . The illness was of brief duration. His only complaint was that he was tired. In harmony with his life he did not

go down to the setting of the sun, but passed away with the rising morn at 4 o'clock.

His last sermon was delivered in Broadway Christian Church [at Louisville, Kentucky], May 29, 1927, on the subject, "The Foundation of the Christian's Hope." It was beautiful as a going away message. The realization of his hopes must be glorious, for he stood on a firm foundation. The things he desired are now wonderfully brought to fruition.

The name of J. B. Briney will live long. His influence for good will go on until it reaches the farthest shore. His loved ones will have only a short time to wait before they will receive him again. When the shadows have grown a little longer, they will be with him again. This will be in the dawning of the morn when all mists are cleared away.

G. W. Nutter.

❖ ❖ ❖

MRS. LUCINDA HOLBERT BRINEY was born in 1838 and died in 1906. She is remembered by some of our older members as a woman of charm and friendliness, who took her full share of responsibility in the work of the women of this church.

Abner Peter Cobb

Pastor 1891-1898

BORN: October 27, 1853, at Somerset, Ohio
DIED: February 11, 1923, at Decatur, Illinois
MARRIED: Marilla Magdalene Dennis
CHILDREN: Ethel Mary Cobb (Mrs. James L.) Adams Jr.; died November 3, 1939
Zoe Cobb (Mrs. Luther Allen) Sommer; Cleveland Heights, Ohio
Ambrose Merle Cobb; died December 10, 1942
Lois Margarita Cobb (Mason); died March 14, 1958
Cyril Malcolm Cobb, Decatur, Illinois
Harold Llewellyn Cobb, Chicago, Illinois
Evelyn Estelle Cobb, Elois Cobb — Twins; born 1892; died 1894
Elise Cobb; born 1894; died 1897
Lillian Irene Cobb (Hobbs); born 1896; Decatur, Illinois

Herbert Georg Studio

Abner Peter Cobb

Herbert Georg Studio

Marilla Magdalene Dennis Cobb

Mr. Cobb's family came to Decatur in 1867. Here he attended school, and while in his teens learned the machinist trade. He was strong in body and vigorous in mind, and made good progress in both lines of work. In those years he was in the school of adversity as well. Graduating at Eureka in 1878 [later returning and earning his A.M.], he entered the ministry. As a pastor he served the church at Normal two periods, at Springfield [Illinois], six years; at Des Moines, Ia., and at San Antonio, Tex. For ten years he served as an efficient evangelist in the United States and Canada. He held successful meetings in Boston, New York City, Minneapolis and other great centers. For fourteen years he has been platform manager at summer Chautauquas. In him industry, large energy and capacity for work, with thirst for knowledge and wide readings, have united in producing a scholar of more than average attainments.[1]

Miss Norma Brown, chairman of the Division of Off-Campus Information and Service at Eureka College, contributes the following story, related to her by Oliver W. Stewart (Eureka, 1890): Cobb had a reputation for being a scintillating orator, but he told about a lecture engagement he filled at Galesburg, Illinois, which did not go to his liking. It was illustrative of the disservice which good friends often impose upon speakers by demanding social occasions for them before their major appearances.

On this occasion in Galesburg, some person of importance arranged a dinner party to exhibit this clever friend. At the dinner party he shone, he sparkled, he scintillated, he was the bright and shining star of the occasion. But when he rose to his major responsibility on the lecture platform he found himself, very much to his own disgust, utterly depleted and his own estimate was that he was a drab disappointment.

The following is from *The Christian-Evangelist,* February 22, 1923, page 248:

On Sunday morning, Feb. 11, 1923, Brother A. P. Cobb passed into life eternal at the age of 69 years. A brief illness of about three weeks, started with a trouble of the heart and terminated in pneumonia. The

[1]Haynes, Nathaniel S., *History of the Disciples of Christ in Illinois, 1915.* Cincinnati, The Standard Publishing Company, p. 498.

place of his birth was Somerset, Ohio, but most of his life had been lived in Illinois. For many years he had made Decatur his home. He graduated from Eureka College in the class of 1878. The year following, he was united in marriage with Maggie M. Dennis who with seven children survive him.

The first pastorate of Brother Cobb was at Washburn, Ill., and then in Petersburg and Normal, Ill.; Des Moines, Ia.; Covington, Ky.; Springfield, Ill. He gave himself to evangelistic work and was called to almost every State of the union for meetings. For a number of years he had lived here at Decatur and ministered to churches near here and served in evangelistic work.

Brother Cobb was a great student. . . . He was blessed with a ready memory and could quote more accurately and extensively than most men. He was an interesting speaker and always brought a most helpful message. He was a ready conversationalist and was at home in almost any group.

During the six years that the writer has been his pastor, he has always been a sympathetic and helpful member.—John R. Golden.

✣ ✣ ✣

MRS. MARILLA MAGDALENE DENNIS COBB was born May 20, 1855, at Decatur, Illinois, and died December 18, 1944, at Decatur, Illinois. She was known to her friends as "Maggie." She graduated from high school at Decatur, Illinois, and attended one semester at Eureka College. She taught several years before her marriage to Mr. Cobb.

At Springfield and elsewhere, she was active in the Daughters of the American Revolution. Her youngest daughter, Mrs. Lillian Cobb Hobbs, of Decatur, Illinois, writes on February 20, 1961: "Mother was a lifetime student—never stopped studying."

Jay Elwood Lynn

Pastor 1898-1902

BORN: November 30, 1870, at Canfield, Ohio
DIED: May 5, 1955, at Claremont, California
MARRIED: Lula Olive Gault, June 30, 1897
CHILDREN: Emerson Lynn
Rachel Lynn (Palmer)
Gault W. Lynn

Herbert Georg Studio

Jay Elwood Lynn

Herbert Georg Studio

Lula Olive Gault Lynn

Jay Elwood Lynn was the third son of Hiram and Rachel Lynn. He spent his childhood in Canton, Ohio, and attended Hiram College from 1890 to 1895, receiving both his A.B. and A.M. degrees. In college he had met Miss Lula Olive Gault, whom he married on June 30, 1897.

He was pastor of the First Christian Church in Mansfield, Ohio, from 1895 to 1898, during which time a new church building was erected. He then came to the First Christian Church, at Springfield, Illinois, May 1, 1898. During Mr. Lynn's pastorate, the congregation decided to establish a new church on the west side of Springfield where a substantial portion of the members lived.

In order to provide a suitable name for the new church, a Certificate of Incorporation was filed December 31, 1901, stating that at a meeting held on December 28, 1901, at which B. R. Hieronymus acted as chairman, the name of this church was changed to "First Christian Church of Springfield," adding:

> Said Christian Church was first organized at Springfield A.D. 1833; incorporated March 10, 1880, and reincorporated as above for the purpose of adopting a distinctive designation.

The certificate was recorded in the office of the County Recorder of Sangamon County December 31, 1901, as document 81143, vol. 152M, page 168.

This change of name cleared the way for a meeting of those who were organizing the new congregation, at which Grandville A. Hulett acted as chairman. The name "West Side Christian Church of Springfield, Illinois," was adopted.

First Christian Church released about two hundred of its members to form the nucleus for the new congregation, and at a cost of $17,000 erected a building at the corner of Edwards and State Streets.

To give prestige and to make sure that the new congregation would go forward under its own power, Mr. Lynn became its first pastor and continued until he resigned to become pastor of the Central Christian Church at Warren, Ohio, beginning June 1, 1904.

On July 24, 1902, Jay Elwood Lynn played center field in a baseball game between the ministers and the lawyers of Springfield. The lawyers won by a score of 17 to 16. The game was for the benefit of the Home for the Friendless. Governor Richard Yates acted as referee.

These hardy athletes are really Springfield ministers and -neys who got together July 24, 1902, to play a baseball game the benefit of the Home for the Friendless at YMCA Park, located west of the Sacred Heart Convent and Academy. tains were T. J. Sullivan for the lawyers and the Rev. Archi- Hall for the ministers. The game attracted 1,000 fans who a total of $400 to watch the attorneys win by a score of 17-16. Richard Yates was guest of honor and served as referee. to right, front row, are the Rev. August Hohl; an unidentified cordia College student; the Rev. J. Elwood Lynn of the First stian Church; Clark B. Shipp; Dr. H. L. Dietz of the YMCA, and Edmund Burk; second row, identification uncertain, believed to be either Rabbi Traugott or Meyer Seeberger; Sidney S. Breese, Rev. Hall of the Congregational Church; Sullivan; Governor Yates; David Griffith, umpire; the Rev. Euclid B. Rogers of the First Baptist Church, and the Rev. Alexander Allen of Christ Episcopal Church; third row, Ensign George B. Smith of the Salvation Army; Robert H. Patton; the Rev. J. B. Rogers of the Third Presbyterian Church; the Rev. T. D. Logan of the First Presbyterian Church; Hugh Graham, George M. Morgan, Ed Dunn, Stuart Brown, John G. Friedmeyer, and Pascal E. Hatch.

In March, 1910, Mr. Lynn moved west to become the minister of the Central Christian Church in Pueblo, Colorado, but resigned in approximately six months because of ill health. He next served the Christian Church at Gill, Colorado. His last full-time pastorate was at Loveland, Colorado, which he was forced to give up in 1917 because of his health. He lived for some years in Boulder, Colorado. In September, 1928, he moved to Claremont, California, where he and his wife spent their remaining years. During this period, he contributed some notable articles to religious publications. He served at various times as trustee of Hiram College and of Eureka College.

He died May 5, 1955, at Claremont, California.

✣ ✣ ✣

MRS. LULA OLIVE GAULT LYNN was born April 9, 1873, at North Jackson, Ohio. Her father was John Gault and her mother was Louisa Maria Johnston Gault. In the fall of 1890, she went to Hiram, Ohio, to a preparatory school, and then on to Hiram College from which she graduated June 24, 1897. During the long period of Mr. Lynn's invalidism, Mrs. Lynn took charge of the business and fiscal affairs. As there was no Christian Church in Claremont, California, the Lynns placed their membership in the First Christian Church at Pomona, California. Mrs. Lynn was prominent in the activities of that church. She was in demand for devotionals, and for talks at conferences and other gatherings. Through her efforts, the Christian Women's Federation at Pomona greatly enlarged its work.

In 1950 she received the "Cross and Crown" award from the First Christian Church of Pomona. The award was planned with the idea of showing appreciation for years of faithful service of the older people who were no longer able to be active in the life of the church.

Mrs. Lynn died June 13, 1958, at Claremont, California.

Hugh Tucker Morrison, Jr.

Copastor 1902-1904

BORN: May 23, 1877, at Buchanan, Michigan
MARRIED: Mary Logan Coleman, June 23, 1908
CHILDREN: None

Herbert Georg Studio

Hugh Tucker Morrison, Jr.

Herbert Georg Studio

Mary Logan Coleman Morrison

In the summer of 1902 two young unmarried men, brothers, Charles Clayton Morrison and Hugh Tucker Morrison, Jr., were called to the pastorate of the First Christian Church, then worshiping in a sanctuary located at Fifth and Jackson Streets.

These young men, only recently graduated from Drake University in 1898 and 1900 respectively, were living in Chicago, where for four years Charles C. Morrison had been pastor of the Monroe Street Christian Church, a church which the younger Morrison, Hugh T., had served during the summer of 1898 as a vacation minister, prior to entering his junior year in college.

The two ministers were called simultaneously to the Springfield pastorate in the relation of copastors. The elder was a graduate student in the Department of Philosophy at the University of Chicago, and it was understood that this situation was not to be disturbed. His residence continued in Chicago, and on weekends he commuted between that city and Springfield to preach at the two Sunday worship services.

The younger brother, Hugh T., lived in the parsonage and assumed all the duties of the pastoral office. The names appeared on the bulletin board and on all church publications as follows:

Rev. Hugh T. Morrison, Jr.
and
Rev. Charles Clayton Morrison, Copastors

Officiating at funerals, solemnizing weddings, administering baptisms, counseling and directing of the various organizations of the church were the official responsibility of the junior minister. All pastoral reports were conveyed by him to the church officials and to the congregation. During the final twelve months of the copastorate the junior minister officiated at 60 funerals and solemnized 55 weddings. During the entire dual ministry he administered the rite of baptism to about 90 candidates.

During the copastorate (1902-1904) there were commissioned from First Church membership three outstanding young people to serve on the mission field. These were Miss Rose Theresa Armbruster to Japan, and Dr. Arthur Paul Wakefield and Mrs. Olive Lindsay Wakefield as medical missionaries to China. Mrs. Wakefield was a sister of Vachel Lindsay, the poet.

A similar event of unusual significance was the congregation's decision to become a Living Link in connection with the Foreign Missionary Society. As a result of this action, Dr. Susie Carson Rijnhart, already a well-known missionary, became the congregation's representative in Tibet.

Since only a relatively small number of Christian churches at that time were assuming such a major obligation, First Church came to have a certain degree of distinction for its missionary vision. The reflex influence from these several representatives in missionary areas was deep and extensive. During 1903 Hugh T. Morrison acted as recording secretary of the American Christian Missionary Society.

At the end of two years, the senior minister requested a leave of absence for three months to complete his work at the University of Chicago. This request was granted by the church on condition that the junior pastor would fill the pulpit during this period. However, the junior minister found that his voice was not equal to the strain of pulpit preaching, and decided to prepare himself for the practice of medicine. The copastorate was terminated at the end of 1904 and the senior minister continued as sole pastor from 1904 until October, 1906. After receiving his M.D. degree from Drake Medical College, Hugh returned to Springfield, where he practiced medicine from 1908 to 1942.

On June 23, 1908, Hugh married Mary Logan Coleman. They made their home in the famed Logan Place, erected by her grandfather, Stephen T. Logan, who was Lincoln's second law partner. The house has been replaced by Memorial Hospital, dedicated in October, 1943.

Dr. Morrison took an active part in public affairs. In 1908 he was called on to give the initial presentation of the particular type of commission form of government which in 1909 was adopted by the city of Springfield as a substitute for the aldermanic form. He lectured on current events under the combined auspices of the Springfield Business and Professional Woman's Club, the Y. M. C. A., and the Y. W. C. A.

During World War I, Dr. Morrison served as a medical officer with the rank of Captain, and lectured on social hygiene in the military camps and cantonments of the United States. Later he became a stated lecturer on social hygiene for the Illinois Board of Health.

In 1937 he was the first president of the Illinois Council of Churches. For over 50 years he has been a trustee of the Disciples Divinity House of the University of Chicago.

He was the author of two small volumes: *Logan Place—a Story of an Ancestral Home,* privately printed in 1938; and *Milton G. Owen, M.D.* (a biography of a noted Springfield physician). He also wrote a copyrighted pamphlet, *A Theory of Pitch and Range in Voice Production,* about 1954.

In 1909 Billy Sunday had held a highly successful revival service in Springfield, in which nearly all the Protestant churches co-operated. Over 4,700 persons "hit the sawdust trail." In 1912 Dr. Morrison wrote "A Religious Survey of Springfield," reflecting the effects of the Billy Sunday series of meetings, which was first published in the *Christian Century.* Later it was printed by Dr. Washington Gladden of Columbus, Ohio, and widely circulated.

Since he retired from medical practice, Dr. Morrison has made his home in Springfield, although he spends much of his time in Florida and in Tucson, Arizona.

❖ ❖ ❖

MRS. MARY LOGAN COLEMAN MORRISON was born February 18, 1880, at Springfield, Illinois, and lived almost all her life in Logan Place, one of the show places of the city and erected by her grandfather, Judge Stephen T. Logan, who was Lincoln's second law partner. Her mother died when she was eleven years old, and she soon became its mistress. Her grandmother, America T. Logan, was not a charter member of this congregation, but united with the church soon after its organization in 1833 during the pastorate of Josephus Hewitt. Stephen T. Logan did not become a member of the church, but actively figured in its progress. He was elected trustee in 1852. In the same year, he was appointed a member of a committee "to make arrangements for a more suitable house of worship," which resulted in the second church building. In 1880 he again served on the building committee for the third church building. He was named as one of the trustees in the original Certificate of Incorporation of "The Christian Church of Springfield, Illinois," in 1880.

Mary was a graduate of Springfield High School in 1898, and of Monticello Seminary, and took courses at the University of Chicago. While yet living in the ancestral home, Mrs. Morrison sponsored a centennial celebration of Logan Place on January 1, 1937. This celebration was participated in not only by local relatives and intimate friends of the family, but also by many from other cities and even from remote states. For this occasion Dr. Morrison wrote the volume, *Logan Place—a Story of an Ancestral Home.* At the evening session, an address was given by Dr. Edgar DeWitt Jones, pastor of Central-Woodward Avenue Christian Church of Detroit, Michigan.

For twelve years, from 1911 to 1923, Mrs. Morrison was an elected member of the Springfield Board of Education. She was president of the Board in 1916-1918. When the present Springfield High School structure was erected at Adams and

New Streets, she officiated as president at the laying of the cornerstone on September 19, 1916.

Since early childhood she was a member of the First Christian Church. In 1898 she was a delegate to the national convention of the Young People's Society of Christian Endeavor at Nashville, Tennessee, and in time occupied almost every position of responsibility in the local church, including membership on the official board and on the building committee for the erection of the present structure. In 1904 she spent several months on a Mediterranean cruise, traveling with Dr. and Mrs. Herbert Lockwood Willett, and visiting Egypt and the Holy Land. From 1924 to 1931 she was an active member of the Board of Directors of the Springfield Y. W. C. A., and again from 1936 to the time of her death. She was an honorary member of the Board from January, 1934, to August, 1936. She was President of the Y. W. C. A. from January, 1926, through December, 1928.

One of the treasures in Logan Place was a copy of Andrea del Sarto's painting of "The Holy Family." It now hangs in the Weaver Lounge[1] of the Y. W. C. A. building.

She wrote a historical sketch of First Christian Church on the occasion of its seventy-fifth anniversary in 1908 and a similar sketch for the ninetieth anniversary of the church in 1923. The latter is in the Illinois State Historical Library.

In January, 1914, Dr. and Mrs. Morrison, as foster parents, took into their home the three small sons of Reverend and Mrs. R. Ray Eldred, who had lost their lives on the Congo mission field of Africa. Although not adopted, the youths voluntarily assumed the surname Morrison, and have been known by that name. They are: Ray Eldred Morrison, Ward Eldred Morrison (killed at Pearl Harbor, December 7, 1941), and Dr. Joseph P. Eldred Morrison of the Smithsonian Institution.

[1]Weaver Lounge in the Y. W. C. A. is named in honor of Mr. and Mrs. I. A. Weaver, members of First Christian Church. Mrs. Weaver was co-chairman of the Building Fund campaign to restore and refurnish the building after the fire of May 8, 1947. She is now a member of the Board of Trustees.

Charles Clayton Morrison

Copastor 1902-1904
Pastor 1905-1906

BORN: December 4, 1874, at Harrison, Ohio
MARRIED: Laurel Scott, October 3, 1906
CHILDREN: Jane Morrison (Mrs. Frederick Reed Dickerson)
Helen Morrison (Mrs. Dr. Bertram G. Nelson, Jr.)

Herbert Georg Studio

Charles Clayton Morrison

Herbert Georg Studio

Laurel Scott Morrison

By W. E. Garrison

Charles Clayton Morrison was the son of Hugh T. and Anna (Macdonald) Morrison. He was ordained to the ministry of Disciples of Christ in 1892, at the age of 18. He held student pastorates while taking his college course at Drake University, which gave him his A.B. degree in 1898. His college record was evidently superior in spite of the demands of work with his churches, for when a chapter of Phi Beta Kappa was formed at Drake many years later and was granted the privilege of extending its membership to include some of its most deserving alumni, he was one of those chosen for this academic honor.

During the years between 1892 and 1906, he held pastorates of Christian churches in Clarinda, Iowa; Perry, Iowa; Chicago (Monroe Street Church); and Springfield, Illinois. His brother, Hugh T. Morrison, Jr., was copastor in the Springfield ministry. Within this period also, and while serving the Monroe Street Church, he was a graduate student in the University of Chicago with a fellowship in the Department of Philosophy (1902-1904).

Morrison always had the courage of his convictions, as his later editorial career amply demonstrated. This quality was given early proof when, with the approval of his board, he made the Monroe Street Church an out-and-out "open membership" church. This was probably his first decisive step on the road of ecumenical activity to which so large a part of his subsequent effort was dedicated. He held that it was folly to expect that the union of Christians could ever be attained on a basis including the agreement of all Christians with the "historic position" of Disciples on baptism, and that it was an equal folly for a church professedly pleading for Christian unity to include in its own conditions of membership an item which was itself a barrier against unity. He held also—and presented this view in a book, *The Meaning of Baptism*—that baptism does not *consist* in immersion, though that was doubtless the original form, and is not necessarily invalid without it. The Monroe Street incident and the publication of these views made Morrison a controversial figure. His convictions on this subject never changed, but it dropped into a subordinate place in his thinking as other and more vital issues arose when, as editor of the *Christian Century,* he again gave proof of his courage and independence in dealing with topics of crucial importance for both church and state. Many who had been his critics in the Monroe Street affair came to admire him as a social prophet and a religious statesman. When he took the platform to give an evening address at the International Convention in Buffalo (1948), he received from the huge audience a prolonged standing ovation unparalleled within this writer's long convention experience.

At the end of this period from 1892 to 1906 and very near the end of his Springfield pastorate, Mr. Morrison married Miss Laurel Scott, on October 3, 1906.

The turning point in Morrison's career was his purchase of the assets of the bankrupt *Christian Century* at sheriff's sale for the reputed sum of six hundred dollars. Since the journal formerly called the *Christian Oracle* had taken its new name with new ownership and management on January 1, 1900, it had pursued a brilliant but erratic course gradually tending downward in circulation, editorial strength, prestige, and financial stability toward the ultimate pit of insolvency. Morrison did not get much for his $600, if that is what it was, and he soon lost most of that, for his reputation as a reckless young radical on the baptism question brought a further shrinkage of the already pathetically short subscription list. The transformation of this moribund midget of a denominational weekly into "an undenominational journal of religion" with world-wide prestige, "the most powerful voice in Protestantism," as it has often been called, is one of the most amazing and dramatic chapters in the history of American journalism.

Dr. Morrison's personal prestige rose with that of his paper. He was editor of the *Christian Century* from 1908 until he retired in 1947 when he put the paper into the very capable hands of Paul Hutchinson, who had been managing editor for almost twenty-five years and had written a large proportion of the editorials. Morrison had founded *The Pulpit* (a monthly publication), in 1929 and edited it until 1956. After the death of Peter Ainslie in 1935, he took over the orphaned *Christian Unity Quarterly* which Ainslie had founded and edited, enlarged it, broadened its coverage, and renamed it *Christendom.* Morrison edited this quarterly until in 1941 he gave it to the World Council of Churches, in whose hands it underwent a further change to make it the *Ecumenical Review,* an official organ of the Council.

His other activities included frequent lecturing: the Rauschenbusch Lectures at Colgate-Rochester Theological Seminary; the Southworth Lectures at Andover-Newton Theological Seminary; the Earle Lectures at the Pacific School of Religion; the Lyman Beecher Lectures at Yale Divinity School; the Swander Lectures at Lancaster Theological Seminary; the William Henry Hoover Lectures on Christian Unity at the Disciples Divinity House, University of Chicago; and intermittent service as professorial lecturer at Chicago Theological Seminary, 1931-1949. He received many honorary degrees: D.D. from Oberlin College, 1923, and from Chicago Theological Seminary, 1928; Litt.D., Syracuse University, 1928; and LL.D., Culver-Stockton College 1933, and Drake University, 1938.

An important chapter in Dr. Morrison's career was his work in support of the outlawry-of-war proposal. This plan for guaranteeing the peace of the world was initiated by Salmon Levinson, a Chicago lawyer. He convinced Morrison, who became the chief journalistic advocate. Together they convinced Senator Borah. Borah convinced the Secretary of State, Frank Kellogg. Kellogg convinced Briand, Premier of France. Hence the Kellogg-Briand pact which was ratified by the governments of many nations. The advocacy of this plan brought Dr. and Mrs. Morrison into close and friendly contact with governmental leaders in various parts of Europe. It also furnished material for many editorials and one book. Of even more significance was Dr. Morrison's personal acquaintance with church leaders throughout the world. He attended all the great ecumenical gatherings beginning with Edinburgh, 1910, where the seeds were planted which ripened into the World Council of Churches.

A complete bibliography of Dr. Morrison's writings would require weeks to compile and pages to print. His books are as follows: *The Meaning of Baptism,* 1914; *Hymns of the United Church* (ed., with H. L. Willett), 1916; *The Daily Altar* (ed. with H. L. Willett), 1918; *The Outlawry of War,* 1927; *The Social Gospel and the Christian Cultus,* 1933; *What Is Christianity?* 1940; *The Christian and the War,* 1942; *The Unfinished Reformation,* 1954.

His present address is 1545 East 60th St., Chicago 37, Ill.

A biographical sketch of Dr. Morrison appears in 20 biennial issues of *Who's Who in America* from Volume 11, 1920-1921, to and including Volume 29, 1956-1957, and again in Volume 31, 1960-1961.

✣ ✣ ✣

MRS. LAUREL SCOTT MORRISON was the daughter of Mr. and Mrs. William Poole Scott. She graduated from Springfield High School in 1894, and from the Springfield Training School for Teachers. She taught from 1894 to 1906 in the Stuart School at Springfield. She was also a voice student, and became one of the recognized vocalists of the city. She was an officer of the Springfield Philharmonic Society, and an active member of the Springfield Choral Union for several years. At that time the usual church choir consisted of a quartet. Although she was not a member of the church she sang alto in the choir at First Christian Church, when Charles Clayton Morrison came as copastor with his brother Hugh. Under the influence of his preaching, she united with the church. She became his wife on October 3, 1906.

Frederick William Burnham

Pastor 1907-1914

BORN: May 7, 1871, at Chapin, Illinois
DIED: January 13, 1960, at Richmond, Virginia
MARRIED: Cenie Allison, October 2, 1895
CHILDREN: None

Herbert Georg Studio

Frederick William Burnham

Herbert Georg Studio

Cenie Allison Burnham

By Beulah Gordon

During the six years from 1907 to 1914 when the present First Christian Church edifice was being constructed, Frederick William Burnham served as pastor and as chairman of the building committee. At his suggestion the building—said to be the most beautiful among the Disciples of Christ—was modeled after Melrose Abbey in Scotland.

Dr. Burnham came to Springfield from Decatur, Illinois, where a new church was built during the six years of his ministry. He left Springfield to answer the call of the Wilshire Boulevard Church of Los Angeles, California. He had scarcely begun his ministry in Los Angeles, when he was named first president of the American Christian Missionary Society (Home Missions). He assumed his duties on December 11, 1914, and remained as chief executive until 1919 when The United Christian Missionary Society was formed. He served the United Society as president until his resignation on December 10, 1929.

During most of his years as president of The United Christian Missionary Society its headquarters were in St. Louis, Missouri, but later were moved to Indianapolis, Indiana.

During 1930, the year following his resignation as president of the U. C. M. S., Dr. Burnham served as pastor of University Park Christian Church, Indianapolis. From 1931 until he retired in 1946 he was pastor of the Seventh Street Christian Church in Richmond, Virginia. He died in Richmond on January 13, 1960.

In a tribute to Dr. Burnham, the Board of Trustees of The United Christian Missionary Society, meeting on January 19, 1960, six days following his death, said:

> Mr. Burnham was not only a recognized leader among Disciples of Christ, he was also a dominant figure in the ecumenical movement.

Mr. Burnham, in addition to his outstanding ability as a preacher, administrator and author, has been characterized as one of the finest presiding officers and parliamentarians ever produced by Disciples of Christ. It was this fact, together with his great and lasting contribution to the work of the church at home and abroad, that caused the board of trustees to name the auditorium of the new wing of the Missions Building, the Frederick W. Burnham Auditorium.

In a letter written on February 11, 1959, Dr. Burnham, in summing up his career, said:

Dear Brother McElroy: In accordance with your communication of February 4, I am submitting herewith a biographical sketch of Mrs. Burnham and myself. I have not made a separate sketch for Mrs. Burnham because our lives and services were so intimately interwoven, except that I have given her college life independently. My reason for entering the ministry was a natural development. I had never contemplated any other life-calling.

I have no comment to make upon my pastorate in Springfield, except to say that memory holds most dear the fellowship of such men as Charles P. Kane, L. H. Coleman, B. R. Hieronymus, A. W. Hillier, G. A. Hulett, Frank A. Drake, Edward Anderson and Henry B. Henkel, and others, and such women as Mrs. George Pasfield, Mrs. Emma Kreider, Mrs. Mary Coleman Morrison, Mrs. I. A. Weaver and many other noble women.

Frederick William Burnham was born of New England parentage in Chapin, Illinois, May 7, 1871. His father was a physician, At the age of 17, he became a railway telegrapher and served the Wabash Railroad at the Union Depot, Hannibal, Missouri, and the Northern Pacific Railroad in Montana. He attended Whipple Academy, the preparatory school of Illinois College, at Jacksonville, Illinois, and went to Eureka for his college work. [While still an undergraduate, he was listed among the members of the faculty for the sessions of 1892-1893 and 1893-1894 as Teacher of Telegraphy and Railroad Bookkeeping in the Business Department.] He graduated from Eureka College in 1895 with an A.B. degree; attended the University of Chicago the summer of 1902 and again in 1931-32. He received the degree of LL.D. from Eureka College in 1915.

In October, 1914, F. W. Burnham was elected president of the American Christian Missionary Society (Home Missions) and visited churches in every state in the United States, Puerto Rico, Canada and Alaska. In 1919 the several missionary societies were united under the United Christian Missionary Society (U. C. M. S.), and F. W. Burnham was elected president successively for the next 10 years in open convention elections.

He was chairman of the Executive Committee of the Federal Council of Churches of Christ in America, 1902-24; delegate to the first preliminary conference on Faith and Order in Geneva, Switzerland, 1920; delegate to the World Conference on Life and Work, Stockholm, Sweden, 1925; delegate to the Federal Conference of Churches of Christ in New Zealand and Australia, 1927-28. In 1928-29 he visited the mission fields of the United Christian Missionary Society in India, China, Japan, and Philippine Islands, in 1925 he toured Russia and Scandinavia for the American Christian Missionary Society; and for the Near East Relief he visited Palestine, Turkey, and Constantinople, now Istanbul. He was a delegate to the Conference of Life and Work in Oxford, England, in 1931.

Other interdenominational responsibilities of Mr. Burnham are listed by the Board of The United Christian Missionary Society as: vice-president of Illinois Christian Endeavor Union, 1902-1904; president of Illinois Christian Endeavor Union, 1904-1906; trustee of Eureka College, 1902-1914; commissioner of World Conference of Faith and Order, 1910-1925; chairman of Commission on Moral and Social Problems of the Universal Christian Conference on Life and Work, 1920-1925; director of World Alliance for International Friendship Through the Churches; director of Near East Relief; member of Council of Boy Scouts of America; and member of Foreign Missions Council and Home Missions Council.

The personnel record, filled out by Dr. Burnham when he was president of the U. C. M. S., states that he was first ordained to the ministry in 1895 upon his graduation from Eureka College, and was again ordained in 1909 by the elders of First Christian Church at Springfield, Illinois.

From February 26, 1909, to April 12, 1909, William A. (Billy) Sunday conducted a union revival service in Springfield, Illinois, during which 4,721 persons "hit the sawdust trail." Each convert was asked to name the Protestant church of his preference. Over 400 cards designated First Christian

Church. Dr. Burnham proceeded to conduct a three-week evangelistic service in this church, resulting in over 300 additions to the church roll, as fruits of the Billy Sunday campaign.

In 1918, while president of The United Christian Missionary Society, Dr. Burnham wrote a book entitled *Unification—The How, What, and Why of The United Christian Missionary Society.* The character and scope of the book are well expressed by Charles S. Medbury in the Introduction:

> As I think of an introductory word for President Burnham's splendid setting forth of the lines of the life and work of the United Christian Missionary Society, a fine expression of A. McLean's comes to mind. Many will recall his saying: "Information is the panacea for both apathy and antipathy."
>
> If our people only knew more of the actual challenges from the whole world field with which our representatives grapple constantly—if there could only be brought home to them personally the heart-cries of missionaries in appealing fields, both at home and abroad—they could not be indifferent to the support of our co-operative work. . . . And so the president has done well to tell the simple story as he has. What he has written should be widely read, and, meantime, those serving us by our call, should have our loving and prayerful support.

He was also the author of *A Missionary Visit to Alaska.*

A biographical sketch of Dr. Burnham appears in *Who's Who in America* in 12 biennial issues, beginning with Volume 15, 1928-1929, to and including Volume 26, 1950-1951.

✣ ✣ ✣

MRS. CENIE ALLISON BURNHAM was born January 28, 1870, at Eureka, Illinois. Her father was a Union soldier in the Civil War, and was a prisoner of war in Libby Prison at Richmond, Virginia. Cenie graduated at Eureka College in 1894 with degrees of A.B. and B.S. She remained another year at Eureka and studied art. In a letter written February 11, 1959, Dr. Burnham said:

She and F. W. Burnham were married October 2, 1895. With her husband she became a world-traveler and an efficient pastor's helper. Together they served pastorates in Carbondale, Illinois, 1901-1907; Springfield, Illinois, First Church, 1907-1914; Los Angeles, California; Wilshire Boulevard Church, 1914; Indianapolis, Indiana, University Park Church, 1930; Richmond, Virginia, Seventh Street Church, 1931-1946; Virginia Rural Churches, 1946-1948; pastor emeritus, Seventh Street Church, Richmond, Virginia, since 1946. On most of Dr. Burnham's world travels Mrs. Burnham accompanied him at her own expense. She died in Richmond, Virginia, October 26, 1955, after 60 years of devoted companionship.

They had no children.

Frank Waller Allen

Pastor 1914-1917

BORN: September 30, 1878, in Trimble County, Kentucky
DIED: December 15, 1936, at Los Angeles, California
MARRIED: Ann Mary Meek
DAUGHTER: Mary Jane Allen (Mrs. Chester Evan Sherwood)

Herbert Georg Studio

Frank Waller Allen

Herbert Georg Studio

Ann Mary Meek Allen

Frank Waller Allen was the son of Frank Gibbs Allen, a Disciple minister and editor, and Nancy Maddux Allen. He attended Kentucky University, now Transylvania, at Lexington, Kentucky, at various periods from 1896 to 1904, but did not graduate. He developed an interest in extracurricular literary activities, such as Lyceum Bureau attractions. Before entering the ministry he was a newspaper reporter with the *Louisville Courier Journal,* and later with the *Kansas City Star.* He became pastor of First Christian Church in 1914, following Frederick William Burnham.

The Christian-Evangelist, May 28, 1914, said:

Springfield, Ill., Calls Frank Waller Allen.—In accepting a call to First Church, Springfield, Ill., Frank Waller Allen, for seven years pastor at Paris, Mo., will take the leadership of one of Illinois' largest churches—a congregation of 800 with a magnificent $125,000 building. His ministry at Paris proved beyond all doubt his fitness for the task before him. . . .

Editorially the "Paris, Missouri, *Mercury*" says:

"Frank Allen is not alone a big preacher, but a big man as well, uniting to a broad culture in books an intimate and sympathetic knowledge of life, and adding to both a capacity for practical achievement and an energy that never tires."

On May 17, 1917, *The Christian-Evangelist* reported:

Frank Waller Allen Resigns at First Church, Springfield, Illinois.—Frank Waller Allen will close a ministry of over three years at First Church, Springfield, Ill., on August 1. A determined effort was made by every member of the church board to induce Bro. Allen to withdraw his resignation, but because the strain of hard work is telling upon his health, Bro. Allen declared this action final.

The *Illinois State Register* of May 7, 1917, said:

Regret over the resignation will be felt throughout Springfield, but close friends were cheered yesterday when, after learning of the resignation, they were given assurance that Mr. Allen will remain a resident of Springfield while continuing and enlarging his literary work. He is in great demand as a lecturer and will fill a number of lecture engagements after retiring from his present church work. He has engaged in some literary work incident to his ministry and has contributed many valuable writings to the world of literature. Mr. Allen's Lyceum work will be managed by the American Bureau of Arts and Travel, of Chicago.

In 1924 the Allens went to California where Mr. Allen gave up the ministry and withdrew from the brotherhood of Disciples of Christ. He devoted full time to the Unity Metaphysical Library and Studio.

Among his books are *My Ships Aground* (1900); *Back to Arcady* (1905); *The Golden Road* (1910); *The Lovers of Skye* (1913); *The Brothers of Bagdad* (1913); *Painted Windows* (1918); *The Great Quest* (1918); *My One Hundred Best Novels* (1919); *Wings of Beauty* (1929); and *Creative Living* (1930).

In 1914 Frank Waller Allen came to Springfield as pastor of the First Christian Church. His views soon proved too liberal and by 1918 he had resigned and was lecturing at the Springfield College of Music and Allied Arts. He left Springfield in 1924 and went to California, where he continued to write and lecture. The last of his books to appear in the Library of Congress catalog was *Creative Living* (Long Beach: Unity Metaphysical Library and Studio, 1930).[1]

At least two of his books were published at Springfield, Illinois, by the Springfield College of Music and Allied Arts—*The Great Quest* (1918) and *Painted Windows* (1918).

The Illinois State Library has two of his books: *The Lovers of Skye* (fiction) and *Painted Windows* (essays). The Illinois State Historical Library has a copy of *Painted Windows.*

❖ ❖ ❖

MRS. ANN MARY MEEK ALLEN was born August 5, 1889, the daughter of Lafayette Meek and Mary Powell Meek, both graduates of Vanderbilt University. Her father was a Methodist minister, and died when she was three months old.

[1]From "Reference Report" in Illinois State Historical Library, dated 5 Nov. 1951.

She and her mother went to live with an uncle, Lewis Powell, a Methodist minister with pastorates in Tennessee and Kentucky. Her grandfather, Zephaniah Meek, was editor and publisher of the *Central Methodist* in Catlettsburg, Kentucky.

She graduated at Millersburg College at Millersburg, Kentucky, with the degree of B.A. She then did graduate work at the University of Chicago, followed by extension work at the graduate level from the University of Illinois.

After attending the University of Chicago, she started a kindergarten class in Springfield, which was subsidized by the PTA until the Board of Education included it as part of the city school system. She continued this work until 1924 when the Allens moved to California.

She returned to Springfield in the early '30's, and accepted a position with the Welfare Department of the Illinois Public Aid Commission, covering Sangamon County. She was listed as social case worker until April, 1942. Then she became a case worker supervisor until 1948, when she went again to California to engage in the same type of work at Los Angeles. The Allens' daughter, Mary Jane Allen, is married to Chester Evan Sherwood. They live in Glendale, California.

While in Springfield she reviewed books for the *Illinois State Journal* for more than a year, and she has done considerable writing on welfare subjects. She writes on November 26, 1960: "I have a very warm feeling for the years I lived in Springfield and the friends I made there, and will always be grateful for my stay in that city."

Her present address is 1513¼ North Hoover Street, Los Angeles 27, California.

William Frederic Rothenburger

Pastor 1918-1927

BORN: March 5, 1874, at Holgate, Ohio

DIED: September 7, 1959, at Denver, Colorado

MARRIED: (1) Kate Parmly Teachout, June 27, 1906; died 1908

Daughter: Ruth Mae Rothenburger (Mrs. Malcolm Stuart Ferguson)

(2) Leila Covert Avery, August 9, 1913; died 1942

Children: Ada Jane Rothenburger (Mrs. E. E. Rogers)

Wilma Rothenburger (Mrs. Warren C. Winkler)

(3) Arlene Dux Scoville (widow of Charles Reign Scoville), August 2, 1943

Children: None

Herbert Georg Studio

William Frederic Rothenburger

Herbert Georg Studio

Leila Covert Avery Rothenburger

William Frederic Rothenburger was born on a farm, the son of Christian William and Catherine J. (Leonhart) Rothenburger. He attended a country school and then walked three and a half miles daily to high school. He graduated from Ohio Normal University in 1898, and received an A.B. degree from Hiram College in 1900. He taught Hebrew while a student there.

In 1907 he received the degree of B.D. from the University of Chicago. In 1932 Eugene Bible College of Spokane University conferred on him the honorary degree of D.D.

He was ordained in 1900 to the ministry of Disciples of Christ. His pastorates were at:

Ashtabula, Ohio, 1900-1905; Irving Park Christian Church, Chicago, 1906-1907; Franklin Circle Christian Church, Cleveland, Ohio, 1908-1918; First Christian Church, Springfield, Illinois, 1918-1927; and Third Christian Church, Indianapolis, Indiana, 1927-1943.

He then married Mrs. Arlene Dux Scoville (third wife) and for ten years they conducted evangelistic campaigns of two or three weeks each in all parts of the country. He placed his membership in the University Park Christian Church, of Indianapolis, Indiana.

He was the first president of the Springfield Council of Churches, which was organized May 23, 1924.

He occupied almost every place of honor and responsibility in the brotherhood. He was a trustee of the Pension Fund of Disciples of Christ in 1931 to 1942; member of board of directors of Flanner House at Indianapolis, Indiana; vice-president of the Board of Church Extension; chairman of the Executive Committee, board of trustees and board of managers of The United Christian Missionary Society; delegate to the Federal Council of Churches; and president of the International Convention of Disciples of Christ in 1934.

He made a study tour of Europe in 1911, and made a tour of the mission fields of the Orient in 1924. He was a fraternal delegate to the Annual Conference of Churches of Christ (Disciples) in Great Britain in 1936.

He was the author of *The Cross in Symbol, Spirit and Worship,* which was published by Stratford Co., Boston, in 1930. A review of the book by J. Edward Moseley, of Indianapolis, Indiana, says:

> This volume was written because of the author's interest in the Cross as a spiritual symbol possessing vital meaning for people in everyday life. Originally, much of the material was used in sermons and addresses.
>
> The Prologue is a meditation. "Part I, Seven Words from the Cross," is a series of homilies. "Part II, The Cross—Symbol and a Spirit," sets forth the early uses and abuses of the Cross and contrasts the Roman Catholic and Protestant interpretations of it. "Part III, The Lord's Supper—In Memory of Him," interprets the Spirit of the Cross from a limited theological view.
>
> Each of the major subjects is introduced by the reproduction of a great religious painting.
>
> The historical research which supports the author's spiritual interpretations reflects the symbolic use of the Cross as an aid to worship as well as its legitimate use in art, architecture, and worship.
>
> While the material, the effort of a busy minister in a large urban church, is not treated exhaustively, it is easy to read and may stimulate further study about the Cross by the conscientious reader.

He also wrote many tracts, besides contributions to religious publications. He was a Mason.

In 1938 his three daughters combined to give a word picture of their father which we quote:

WE GO INTO A HUDDLE CONCERNING DAD

Ruth, Jane, and Wilma Rothenburger

Frequently people seem to think that a minister has little to do but preach one or two sermons a week. If they could shadow our dad for several days, they would change their ideas decidedly, because a busier man would be hard to find, as is true no doubt of every minister who is deeply consecrated to his work. From firsthand information we are fully conscious of the fact that the job of being a minister, especially in a large city church, is one that takes every hour of the day. He is not only preacher, but also pastor, administrator, and counselor, and his time is everyone's but his own.

Luckily Dad's tremendous energy makes it possible for him to cope with all the demands made upon him. To him the ministry is all absorbing and in his estimation there is no work so inspiring and fruitful. We once heard him say to a guest of ours that though one never becomes rich in the ministry, there is no other work that pays higher dividends in personal gratification. So he is never too busy to be of help to someone and is glad to leave early for appointments to drop in on families where there is sickness or death. He writes to welcome new arrivals to the city, to congratulate graduates, and to wish brides happiness. His personal and sincere interest in everyone is a fundamental reason why he is generally loved and highly respected. If you want to know how many friends he has, ask the postman.

And sermons? Dad realizes that the pulpit is his one greatest opportunity to reach his people. A sermon brews in the back of his head for weeks sometimes before it is dictated. All the while he is reading much, both in his study and at the library. He thinks every dollar paid for books is well spent—that goes for the whole family as well as for himself. Once we tried to persuade him that he should have a radio in his car to entertain him while driving. Then it was we learned that in those odd moments between calls and meetings he formulates his sermons. His delivery is forceful and he seldom refers to his notes, which consist of a single card of handwritten outline. One Sunday morning a sheet of paper was blown from the pulpit and later several of the congregation spoke of the fear they had had that he might not get through his sermon, but the paper had not been missed. He is often told how much his sermons are appreciated and we feel that he has a happy faculty for saying the right thing in a helpful and tactful way.

In all his efforts he has had the assistance of a wife who has entered wholeheartedly into the work herself and is just as generous with her talent and time. We often laugh about the woman who said so aptly that she just couldn't help telling them how much they reminded her of a pair of mules—they worked together so well.

We think Dad is well rounded in more ways than the one we joke him about. He follows current events closely, belongs to clubs, and takes part in many activities. We know no one who more enjoys meeting people and making chance acquaintances. He strikes up a conversation with all those with whom he comes in contact and is always the first to make friendly overtures. He learns about the barbering business while in the barber's chair, and all the problems of a porter while on the train. This genuine interest in everyone has gone a long way in encouraging people to come to him with all their troubles, confident that they will have an interested and helpful advisor.

Dad is dignified upon occasion but he is also capable of throwing off that dignity. Bedtime romps have passed with the years, but hardly a dinner hour goes by without at least one or two grown daughters piling into his lap to give him a bear hug during the after-dinner chat.

All three of us feel that no one could do a better job of being a father than our own has done. No doubt, at some time or other the razzing that ministers' children come in for has gone a little against the grain but being P. K.'s (Preachers' Kids) has all been on the profit side. When this article was requested the most youthful of the trio remarked, "I wouldn't have been born in any other family for the world even if I didn't get to dancing school or own a bike." And that put it into a nutshell for all of us.

Our parents have always given us all the advantages within their power to give: close medical attention, advantages of books and travel, and contacts with interesting people and things. The full rich life they have had they have shared with us. We have been reared in an atmosphere of optimism and unity, and there is no feeling like that of the pride we have when even total strangers say to us, "Oh, yes, I know your father and mother and admire them very much." Their wide acquaintanceship and extensive travel have meant much in our lives, and Gandhi, Kagawa, and Adolph Keller are not mere names but personalities made very real to us. But of just as much interest to us is the fact that their contacts cut through all the strata of society as well.

Rearing a family is never an easy proposition but our dad always finds time to listen to our troubles and help us straighten out our individual problems with a patience and understanding which have been invaluable to us. He has such an optimistic and buoyant philosophy of life and such fine idealism that "life with Father" has been a constant inspiration.[1]

Mr. Rothenburger attended the International Convention of Christian Churches (Disciples of Christ) at Denver in August, 1959. At the opening session he took his place on the platform with the other living past presidents of the International Con-

---

[1]From *My Dad—Preacher, Pastor, Person.* Edited by George A. Campbell and J. Edward Moseley (St. Louis: Bethany Press, 1938), pp. 136-140.

vention who were presented to the audience. Perhaps the exertion of the trip was too much. Without leaving Denver he died September 7, 1959. Funeral services were held at the University Park Christian Church at Indianapolis, Indiana. Burial was in Crown Hill Cemetery at Indianapolis.

A biographical sketch of Dr. Rothenburger appears in *Who's Who in America,* in 10 biennial issues, from Volume 18, 1934-1935, to and including Volume 27, 1952-1953.

⁘ ⁘ ⁘

(1) MRS. KATE PARMLY TEACHOUT ROTHENBURGER was the daughter of Mr. and Mrs. A. R. Teachout of Cleveland, Ohio. He was a leading businessman in Cleveland, and was known as a liberal giver to the support of Disciples of Christ in northern Ohio. She was born in Cleveland and graduated from high school there. She married Mr. Rothenburger June 27, 1906. There was one daughter, Ruth Mae, who became the wife of Malcolm Stuart Ferguson. Mrs. Kate Rothenburger died in 1908.

⁘ ⁘ ⁘

(2) MRS. LEILA COVERT AVERY ROTHENBURGER had been a teacher in Cleveland high schools for some years before she married Mr. Rothenburger on August 9, 1913. She was with him in Springfield during his pastorate at this church. Two daughters were born to them in Springfield—Ada Jane (Mrs. E. E. Rogers) and Wilma or Billie (Mrs. Warren C. Winkler). Mrs. Winkler writes: "I always had the feeling that Springfield was my mother's favorite career spot."

Resolutions of regret and appreciation were adopted by the congregation when Mr. Rothenburger resigned in 1927 to become pastor of the Third Christian Church at Indianapolis, Indiana, including:

And, be it further resolved:

That in the departure of Mrs. W. F. Rothenburger the women's council, the church, and its organizations lose a brilliant and faithful co-worker, and a woman of fine and lovely character; and that we shall miss her very greatly, and know that we shall not easily fill her place with one so devoted and earnest in all the departments of the church.

The resolutions are signed by James B. Searcy, chairman, Erma Templeman and Philo B. Kane, committee. Alongside the signatures is the following:

The above resolutions were passed on Wednesday eve, June 29, 1927, and are to be recorded in the Archives of the church.

J. B. S.
of Committee.

Mrs. Leila Rothenburger died in 1942.

✣ ✣ ✣

(3) MRS. ARLENE DUX SCOVILLE ROTHENBURGER was the widow of Charles Reign Scoville, who was one of the most successful evangelists among Disciples of Christ. She married him in 1906. Together they spent about a year in Australia and visited twenty-three foreign countries singing and speaking. He died in 1938. On August 2, 1943, she married Dr. Rothenburger. Her education was principally in music. She holds both bachelor and master's degrees from the Chicago Conservatory of Music, and was a private student of Oscar Saenger and John Dennis Mehan in New York. From 1943 to 1952 she and Dr. Rothenburger held short evangelistic campaigns, usually of two weeks each, in many parts of the country. She was soloist and music director, while he did the preaching. Mrs. Rothenburger estimates that upward of 500 additions resulted. She lives at 3751 Central Avenue in Indianapolis, Indiana, and is still active in music.

Clark Walker Cummings

Pastor 1928-1937

BORN: June 6, 1885, at Grand Haven, Michigan
DIED: January 14, 1950, at St. Louis, Missouri
MARRIED: Bess Eva Durbin, February 14, 1911
CHILDREN: Gail Cummings (Mrs. John E. Raber)
Jean Cummings (Mrs. Charles E. Wilson)

Herbert Georg Studio

Clark Walker Cummings

Herbert Georg Studio

Bess Eva Durbin Cummings

Clark Walker Cummings attended Eureka College during the school years 1907-1910, but did not graduate. Later he attended the University of Chicago Divinity School during the summer of 1912 and the summer quarter of 1913, without receiving a degree. He was ordained in 1908. He held pastorates at Knoxville and Ipava, Illinois; Janesville, Wisconsin; Flint, Michigan; and Evanston, Illinois, from which place he came to the First Christian Church in Springfield in 1927. He resigned to accept a call to become executive secretary of the Metropolitan Church Federation at St. Louis, Missouri, on May 1, 1937. The *Illinois State Journal,* on February 22, 1937, said editorially:

The new field to which he will shortly dedicate himself at St. Louis will afford him perhaps a broader opportunity for exercise of the high quality of spiritual leadership which has marked his service in Springfield. His genial personality, his kindliness of manner, his charitable impulses and activities and his lofty conception of the Christian ministry both within and without the church will afford him there, as they have here, the assurance of an extraordinary degree of usefulness to the cause of religion in a much larger community.

The Christian-Evangelist of May 13, 1937, said:

Did you ever see a sleeping giant come to life? That is the thing which has been happening in St. Louis during the days of preparation for the coming of Clark Cummings, of Springfield, Illinois, to be the new secretary of the Metropolitan Church Federation. The city has been districted into 13 districts with officers and councils in each one. All of this is an attempt to spread the work of the Federation throughout every part of the city and to the very last church, small or large. This re-organization has more potential power in facing up to community enterprises than any ever devised. The Disciples of Christ of St. Louis have always been active in the Federation and two of our ministers, Ralph E. Alexander and Maurice W. Fogle, have been elected chairmen in their respective districts. Thus the new secretary is getting the endorsement and the support of the people of our own brotherhood. Mr. Cummings, as secretary, attended his first meeting of the advisory board of the Federation on Friday, April 30. A city-wide reception is being given for him and his family on the evening of May 13 in St. John's M. E. Church.

He had been previously appointed by the International Convention of Disciples of Christ as one of ten delegates to the Universal Conference on Life and Work to be held at Oxford, England, on July 12 to 26, 1937, and he attended, visiting England, Scotland, and Ireland.

His immediate duties at St. Louis were to give attention to over 300 churches and to preach twice a week at various St. Louis churches. His offices were in the downtown Y.M.C.A.

In 1939 Dr. Cummings led a number of church and civic groups in a fight for larger relief appropriations by the state for the unemployed. In 1941 he denounced slums in St. Louis as the worst in the United States. He assailed the "better classes" for tolerating slum conditions, and organized a cooperative religious program to combat the evil effect of slums. In September, 1949, he was named a trustee of the St. Louis Council on World Affairs.

On April 30, 1947, a special meeting of the executive board of the Federation was held with Dr. Cummings as the guest of honor, to observe the tenth anniversary of his tenure. A resolution was adopted by the board that "he has given ample demonstration of noble character and Christian Spirit," and that his leadership "was an inspiration through these ten years of growth in service and unity."

He died in his sleep January 14, 1950, The *St. Louis Post-Dispatch* of January 15, 1950, said editorially:

CLARK WALKER CUMMINGS

Clark Walker Cummings' name became thoroughly known to St. Louis when he led a campaign against illegal arrests, suppression of free speech and police brutality which occurred in the deep depression. This was characteristic of the man who for 12 years was executive secretary of the Metropolitan Church Federation. He took his pulpit where he found it.

He found it close to home in his struggle against political interference in the city schools. He found it in Illinois in opposing bills to take the franchise from men on relief. He found it across the nation in assailing the "better classes" for tolerating slums. On widely assorted issues, from race relations to Palestine, he helped those to whose race and religion he did not belong, as he helped his own.

St. Louis reveres the memory of Clark Walker Cummings because he was a journeyman minister. He worked hard at Christianity. And if anyone should think that description undignified, Mr. Cummings would not have found it so. For of him it could be said:

> Whosoever will be great among you, shall be your minister; and whosoever of you will be the chiefest, shall be servant of all.

MRS. BESS EVA DURBIN CUMMINGS was born November 2, 1890, at Cordova, Illinois, and died August 12, 1954, at St. Louis, Missouri. She attended business college at Galesburg, Illinois. She was married February 14, 1911, to Clark Walker Cummings. At Springfield she taught the Pensee Class in the Bible school, and was active in P. E. O. She served as board member of the Springfield Y.W.C.A. in 1935 and 1936. Also, she had an active part in interdenominational work among women.

Charles Benson Tupper

Pastor 1937-1951

BORN: January 20, 1890, in Harrison County, Iowa
MARRIED: Grace Elizabeth Van Vlack, June 23, 1915
DAUGHTER: Rachael Evelyn

Herbert Georg Studio

Charles Benson Tupper

Herbert Georg Studio

Grace Elizabeth Van Vlack Tupper

Dr. Tupper served a pastorate of fourteen years, from 1937 to 1951, the longest in the history of First Christian Church.

He attended school at Woodbine, Iowa, high school; Drake University, A.B., 1914; and University of Chicago, A.M., 1923. In 1944 Drake University conferred on him the honorary degree of D.D.

He was ordained to the ministry in 1914 in the University Christian Church at Des Moines, Iowa. His pastorates prior to Springfield were at Sioux Falls, South Dakota, 1914-1920; Milwaukee, Wisconsin, 1920-1923; Boulder, Colorado, 1923-1927; and Warren, Ohio 1927-1937.

During Dr. Tupper's pastorate the church debt, which had been carried since the erection of the present building, was paid in full. Rotation in terms of office for the elders was established, as it already existed for the deacons. In 1946 Dr. Tupper won the championship in the squash tournament of the Springfield Y.M.C.A. He served two terms of three years each, from 1940 to 1946, as a director of the Y.M.C.A. and was a member of the National Council of the Y.W.C.A. Among other offices he was one of the vice-presidents of the International Convention of the Disciples of Christ in 1938, the year the assembly met in Denver, Colorado.

Professionally, he is a member of the American Association of University Professors and of the American Association of Theological Professors.

He was active in public affairs of all sorts in Springfield, which partly accounts for the fact that he was honored by election to the Thirty-third Degree in Masonry. The Masons of the church raised a fund to pay the expenses of Dr. and Mrs. Tupper to Philadelphia where he went to receive the degree in 1950.

He is the author of a book, *Called—In Honor,* published

by Bethany Press in 1949. The *Christian-Evangelist* of December 28, 1949, says editorially:

> Recently there has appeared a significant book in this field, *Called—in Honor,* written by Charles B. Tupper, pastor of First Church, Springfield, Ill. In a broad sense it is an interpretation of the code adopted by the Disciples ministers. Mr. Tupper undertakes to discuss frankly the many difficult ethical problems which confront the minister as he endeavors to live up to the high calling to which he has devoted his life. The demands upon the minister for high ethical standards, by the very nature of his calling, are severe since the effectiveness of his message is dependent upon the application which he himself makes of the ethical teaching he proclaims.
>
> Mr. Tupper throws light upon many a dark corner of ethical action of particular concern to the Christian minister. He weighs the minister's attitude toward his predecessor, toward the ministers of other communions, the keeping of personal confidences, honesty in the expression of convictions, industry in the performance of duties.

A former pastor of this church, Dr. Jay Elwood Lynn (1898-1902), wrote from Claremont, California, to Dr. Tupper saying:

> It was my very best Christmas gift for many reasons, one of them being because it is such a fine book and breathes such a fine spirit through all its pages. You may well be proud of it and all of us are proud of you for having written it.
>
> The kind paragraph on pages 99 and 100 about a certain "fellow minister" speaks to me not of anything that I ever did but rather of your own great ability to appreciate the very little things of life.

Dr. Edgar DeWitt Jones wrote:

> It is unique. There isn't anything just like it in the literature of the Disciples. It is a book that is needed. . . . The ministerial code of ethics in your Appendix is high and exacting, but it is not too high, and it is not too exacting. It is a code which should be accepted by all comrades of the Majestic Fraternity.

A tribute from a neighboring Catholic prelate is worth quoting in full, both because of its contents and because it reflects the standing which Dr. Tupper enjoyed among the other religious bodies in Springfield:

CATHEDRAL OF THE IMMACULATE CONCEPTION
524 East Lawrence Avenue
Springfield, Illinois

November 14, 1949

The Reverend Charles B. Tupper
First Christian Church
Springfield, Illinois

Dear Doctor Tupper,

Congratulations, in the sense of thanks to you for the delightful two hours given me in reading your "Called—In Honor." I find myself in full agreement with most you have written. The evident sincerity in which all of it is written makes it inspiring reading.

The thought in your statement on page 148, "Definitive Christian faith never exorcises Christlike love," impresses me as one of your best—notwithstanding the unusual meaning given the word, "exorcise." I can't imagine any evil spirit in Christlike love. My old teacher of rhetoric would have delighted in that sentence not only for its basic Christian thought but as a classic in ellipsis.

Count me a pre-publication subscriber to the next work of your facile pen.

With all good wishes, I am,

Yours sincerely,
JNO. B. FRANZ
Rt. Rev. Msgr. Jno. B. Franz

Dr. Tupper left Springfield in 1951 to become professor of Applied Christianity in the College of the Bible at Drake University. He was presented to the University Community there in a service of introduction October 19, 1951, at which Dr. Tupper gave an address on "When Dreams Come True." A reception in honor of the Tuppers followed, attended by 150 persons. The name of the institution was subsequently changed from "College of the Bible" to "Drake Divinity School."

He was a member of the Board of Managers of the United Christian Missionary Society from 1944 to 1954, and was chairman of the Board in 1947-1948. He was a member of the Board of Trustees of the U. C. M. S., 1944-1950.

A letter of August 9, 1961, from W. B. Blakemore, Dean, telling of Dr. Tupper's service as a member of the Board of

Trustees of the Disciples Divinity House of the University of Chicago, says:

> He was elected to membership on the Board on August 25, 1947. His letter of resignation was accepted on February 24, 1956. Mr. Tupper resigned from the Board because in assuming a faculty position at the Divinity School of Drake University, he was, in some sense, accepting a position at a competitor institution and he felt that there would be incongruity in his retaining a position on the Board of Trustees of Disciples Divinity House. Disciples Divinity House was certainly fortunate to enjoy almost a decade of Mr. Tupper's service and interest on its Board.

He asks to be remembered as the organizer and teacher of the Forum Class in the Bible school. Originally it was known as the "Young Married People's Class"—but time passes.

He also recalls that at Springfield he changed to preaching without notes.

In 1958, when First Christian Church celebrated the 125th anniversary of its organization on April 23, 1833, the program provided that Dr. Tupper should preach on the preceding Sunday, April 19. This was followed by the church dinner on Thursday evening, April 23, 1958.

In June, 1960, Dr. Tupper reached retirement age at the Drake Divinity School, and has since engaged in supply preaching. For three and a half months he preached at the two services each Sunday at the University Christian Church at Des Moines, Iowa, during the pastor's illness. He also served as ad interim pastor at South Bend, Indiana, and at St. Joseph, Missouri. His present address is 4225 Adams Avenue, Des Moines 10, Iowa.

✣ ✣ ✣

MRS. GRACE ELIZABETH VAN VLACK TUPPER was born October 4, 1891, in Cass County, Iowa. She graduated from Simpson College at Indianola, Iowa, with the degree of A.B.

After teaching one year in the high school at Cumberland, Iowa, she married Charles B. Tupper on June 23, 1915. They have one daughter, Rachael, who is on the staff of the research department of the Ohio Farm Bureau at Des Moines, Iowa.

While living in Springfield, Mrs. Tupper was for several years a member of the Board of Directors of the Young Women's Christian Association, and served as its president two terms, in 1946 and 1947.

Harry McCuan Davis

Pastor 1951-1955

BORN: May 8, 1909, at Fulton, Kentucky

MARRIED: Mary Kathleen Trover, December 27, 1933

CHILDREN: Jane Anne Davis (Lollis)—Washington, D. C.
Nancy Trover Davis—Hopkinsville, Kentucky

Herbert Georg Studio

Harry McCuan Davis

Herbert Georg Studio

Mary Kathleen Trover Davis

Harry McCuan Davis is the son of Mr. and Mrs. Horace Cardwell Davis. He attended grade and high schools at Memphis, Tennessee. He received the degree of A.B. at Transylvania College in 1933, and Bachelor of Divinity degree at the College of the Bible in 1935. For three years during World War II he was a chaplain of the Armed Services. His pastorates have been at Greenville, Kentucky; Crestwood, Kentucky; and Central Christian Church, New Albany, Indiana. While at New Albany he was chairman of the committee on Christian Education for the State of Indiana, 1948-1950.

He served as pastor of First Christian Church of Springfield, Illinois, from November, 1951, through June 1, 1955. During that time the education building was remodeled at a cost of $14,500.00 to provide additional class rooms for the Bible school.

While at Springfield he was twice elected president of the Illinois Council of Churches, in 1953 and 1954. For three years he was a member of the Committee on Reorganization of the work in Illinois. For two years he was a member of the Committee on the Ministry of Illinois.

He next became pastor of First Christian Church at Hopkinsville, Kentucky, where he supervised the relocation of the church and the construction of a new church structure costing $450,000.00 which was dedicated November 9, 1958. Since 1958 he has served continuously as chairman of the Board of Trustees and Executive Committee of the Disciples of Christ Historical Society at Nashville, Tennessee. In July, 1961, he was re-elected as trustee for a term of three years, and was also re-elected Chairman of the Board. He was a member of the Board of Directors of the Board of Church Extension at Indianapolis, and member of the Coordinating Council of the state of Kentucky, 1957-58-59. For over ten years he has been a member of the Committee on Recommendations of the International Convention. He has served as academic and administrative dean in Young People's Conferences in fifteen states, including Tennessee, Kentucky, Virginia, West Virginia, North Carolina, Florida, Mississippi, Oklahoma, Illinois, Indiana, Iowa, and other states.

Harry M. Davis shares in the credit for our collection of portraits of former pastors and missionaries and wives, whose biographies are presented here. The idea took form as a result of conferences between Dr. Davis and the church historian in 1954. Dr. Davis initiated the quest for portraits by applying to the Disciples of Christ Historical Society, which forwarded eleven photographs as a beginning. He continued to promote the project as long as he remained pastor.

✣ ✣ ✣

MRS. MARY KATHLEEN TROVER DAVIS was born June 18, 1912, in Hopkins County, Kentucky. She is the daughter of Mr. and Mrs. Barton C. Trover, who now reside at Earlington, Kentucky. After grade and high schools, she attended Transylvania College two years, and took special work in the College of the Bible. At Springfield she taught a class in the Junior Department of the Bible school, and sang in the choir. She was active in the Y.W.C.A., serving on various special committees. She is now vice-president of the Ministers' Wives of the Disciples of Christ of Kentucky.

James Nicholas Gibble

Pastor 1955-1957

BORN: July 30, 1889, in Cartret County, North Carolina
MARRIED: Ella Jane Payne, June 19, 1913
CHILDREN: William Theodore Gibble
Neva Lee Gibble (Oldefest)

Herbert Georg Studio

James Nicholas Gibble

Herbert Georg Studio

Ella Jane Payne Gibble

James Nicholas Gibble is the son of William John and Jennie Gibble. His father was a pioneer preacher among the Christian Churches of eastern North Carolina. His mother was of Dutch descent, coming from Holland when but sixteen years of age. Two years after her landing, she was married to an American twenty years her senior, and to them were born seven sons and five daughters. James was one of the three sons who heard the call of the ministry. His son, William Theodore, constitutes the third generation in the ecclestiastical line.

Mr. Gibble received both his A.B. and M.A. degrees from Phillips University at Enid, Oklahoma, and was ordained to the Christian ministry on May 25, 1917. His career has been strictly pastoral, preaching for Disciples of Christ in Oklahoma, Kansas, and Illinois. During the forty-four years of this constant ministry, he has served in eight different pastorates, including Maywood Christian, Oklahoma City, Oklahoma; Central Park Christian, Topeka, Kansas; and First Christian, Moline, Illinois. This ministry extended into many activities of brotherhood life such as presidency of the Kansas Christian Missionary Society; secretaryship of the Oklahoma Christian Missionary Convention; treasurership of Oklahoma Ministers' Institute; membership on Committee on Recommendations of the International Convention; membership on Executive Board of the Oklahoma City Council of Churches; vesper speaking and teaching in youth conferences; activity in civic clubs and community organizations; 32nd degree Mason.

Mr. Gibble retired from his active ministry in August, 1954. His services continued in ad-interim pastorates. The second of these ministries brought him to the First Christian Church of Springfield, Illinois. This pastorate extended for twenty months during which time 228 members were added to the membership at regular services. Missions giving maintained the ten per cent annual gain over the previous year according to the asking of the brotherhood for a ten-year program of advance then in progress.

He writes (October 25, 1959):

> That the Holy Spirit was enriched in the life of that great and beloved congregation seemed evident, and both the preacher and the congregation rejoiced in the fellowship of Christ and of one another in this short season. The preacher freely testifies of the glory of this church, and ever lifts up his heart in prayer and praise for the continued strength of these people.

✣ ✣ ✣

MRS. ELLA JANE PAYNE GIBBLE was born March 1, 1888, near Bowling Green, Kentucky, and died October 12, 1960, at Enid, Oklahoma.

She was the daughter of Theodore S. and Minnie Payne. She pioneered to Oklahoma with her parents in 1900. In 1907, the first year of that institution's existence she enrolled in Phillips University at Enid, Oklahoma. Its first president, whom she knew personally, was Ely V. Zollars, who had been pastor of this church in 1885-1888. There she obtained her education and higher religious training. She was married to James N. Gibble on June 19, 1913.

Not long before her death, Mr. Gibble wrote:

> Mrs. Gibble often expressed her joy in their chosen profession, having supervised and taught in the several departments of the church. She served on the Board of Managers of the United Christian Missionary Society. She was on the State Boards of the Women's Missionary Societies of Oklahoma, Kansas, and Illinois; dean of women and teacher in more than forty Youth Summer Conferences; a popular speaker on missionary programs and Institutes.
>
> Mrs. Gibble cherished the happy remembrances of the Springfield ad-interim pastorate; the holy beauty of the church's sanctuary, the kindly hands of Christian people whose love and friendliness gave life a fuller meaning. She with her husband feel afresh the heavenly benediction of God granted no less at the even-tide than in life's morning. She, too, offers her prayer of blessing.

Beryl Sales Kinser

Pastor 1957-

BORN: June 17, 1910, in Wayne County, Iowa

MARRIED: Ann Benton Elder, June 20, 1935

CHILDREN: David Everett Kinser, born November 12, 1938, Hannibal, Missouri

Jane Ann Kinser, born December 16, 1940, Clarksville, Tennessee

John Cameron Kinser, born February 12, 1945, Clarksville, Tennessee

Herbert Georg Studio

Beryl Sales Kinser

Herbert Georg Studio

Ann Benton Elder Kinser

In December, 1956, the congregation called Dr. Beryl Sales Kinser, then at Youngstown, Ohio, to become the pastor of the First Christian Church in Springfield beginning March 1, 1957.

The effectiveness of Dr. Kinser's ministry is reflected in the growth of the church. Eight hundred and thirty seven new members have been received into the church, 255 of these by confession of faith and Christian baptism. The church budget has grown from $44,000 to $103,000 and outreach giving for missions, education, and benevolence has increased from $17,-567 to $26,495. Since 1957 the church has purchased three properties immediately south of the sanctuary for a total of $113,000. This is the only available area for parking or expansion.

Our pastor is active in ecumenical and community affairs. A past president of the Springfield Council of Churches, he is currently president of the Ministerial Association of Springfield and Sangamon County. He is a member of the Springfield Kiwanis Club and serves in programs of the United Community Services, Y.M.C.A., Boy Scouts of America, and other civic organizations. He is a member of the Springfield Human Relations Commission and chaplain in the office of Civil and Defense Mobilization.

Dr. Kinser's Masonic affiliations include membership in St. Paul's Lodge No. 500, A. F. & A. M., Elwood Commandery No. 6, K. T., and Abe Lincoln High-Twelve Club. At the meeting of the Grand Lodge in Chicago on October 7, 1961, he was installed as the Right Worshipful Grand Orator of the M. W. Grand Lodge of A. F. & A. M. of Illinois.

Beryl Sales Kinser, son of David C. and Mary Sales Kinser, was reared on the Iowa farm which had been homesteaded by his grandfather, Samuel J. Kinser, in 1853. His Alma Mater, Culver-Stockton College, awarded him the Doctor of Divinity degree on January 25, 1957, with the following citation by Dean John B. Alexander who presented him to President Fred Helsabeck for the award:

President Helsabeck: Beryl Sales Kinser graduated as valedictorian of his class from Promise City, Iowa, High School in 1927; received the degree of Bachelor of Arts from Culver-Stockton College in 1931; and the degree of Bachelor of Divinity from Vanderbilt University School of Religion in 1934.

While in college he was active in athletics, forensics, music, and dramatics. He was honor representative of the junior class, president of the Ministerial Association and a winner of the Lund Debating Prize. While at the graduate school, he was president of the junior class, senior class and Campbell Club, and received the Founders' Medal, the highest scholastic honor, at commencement.

He was ordained to the Christian ministry in 1931 by the Canton, Missouri, Christian Church. He held pastorates as a student at Salem, Santa Fe, Mendon, Oakwood, and Montgomery City, Missouri; and at Columbia and Nashville, Tennessee. Since graduating from the seminary he has been pastor of the First Christian Church at Monroe City, Missouri; and at Clarksville, Tennessee, and for the past eleven years of Central Christian Church at Youngstown, Ohio.

In the work of our brotherhood he has served as chairman of adult work, and of the Ordination Council for District 4, Ohio; and as Ohio representative for the Historical Society of the Disciples of Christ. He has been a member of the Ohio State Commission on Men's Work, the Ohio State Committee of Hiram College. He has served on the faculty of Young People's Summer Conferences in Missouri and Tennessee. He has been a member from Missouri, Tennessee, and Ohio of the Committee on Recommendations, International Convention. He has been a member of the Board of Directors of the International Convention from 1953 to 1957.

He has been active in ecumenical relations in Youngstown and in Ohio, and has been a delegate to the National Council and World Council of Churches. He has been engaged in such community activities as Red Cross, Boy Scouts, Y.M.C.A., Kiwanis and P.T.A.

For his masterful and inspiring demonstration of the life of a Christian pastor, preacher, and churchman at his best, and for his extensive contribution to our brotherhood and the cause of human betterment, Beryl Sales Kinser has been recommended by the faculty and approved by the Board of Trustees of Culver-Stockton College for the degree of Doctor of Divinity. I request that you confer upon him this degree.

In seminary at Vanderbilt University School of Religion, where he was graduated with the B.D. degree in 1934, he received the Founder's Medal for scholarship, the highest student award given by the university. He had served as president of both the junior and senior classes, as a member of the Student Activity Union and as president of the Vanderbilt Campbell Club.

Following his graduation from Vanderbilt, he became pastor of the Christian Church in Montgomery City, Missouri. This was followed by a ministry of almost five years in Monroe City, Missouri. He then was pastor at Clarksville, Tennessee, for seven years, and of the Central Christian Church, Youngstown, Ohio, for eleven years, before coming to Springfield.

As president of the Ministerial Association in Clarksville, Tennessee, he arranged the first interfaith and interracial meeting in the history of the city, with Negroes and whites, Catholics, Jews, and Protestants participating. By contract between the B. F. Goodrich Tire and Rubber Co. and the labor union, all unresolved disputes between labor and management were subject to final arbitration by a board consisting of three persons, one to be designated by management, one by the union, and the other to be Beryl S. Kinser. While in Clarksville, Dr. Kinser served as associate editor of *The Tennessee Christian,* and as Tennessee correspondent for *The Christian-Evangelist.*

Dr. Kinser has attended twenty-four assemblies of the International Convention of Christian Churches (Disciples of Christ) and has served as a delegate member of the Recommendations Committee from the states of Missouri, Tennessee, Ohio, and Illinois. He served from 1953 to 1957 on the Board of Directors of the International Convention and became chairman of the Administrative Year Book Publication, and Headquarters Relocation Committees. He attended the assemblies of the World Convention of Churches of Christ (Disciples) in Buffalo, New York, in 1950, in Toronto, Canada,

1955, and in Edinburgh, Scotland, in 1960, where he was elected to the Central Study Committee in preparation for the 1965 assembly to be held in Puerto Rico.

In addition to the many responsibilities he has accepted in the organizational structures of his own communion in the various states where he has served, Dr. Kinser was a visiting delegate accredited by the Ohio Council of Churches and the Youngstown Council of Churches to the Constituting Convention, National Council of Churches, Cleveland, Ohio, 1950; Biennial Assembly, National Council of Churches, Denver, Colorado, 1952; and the Assembly of the World Council of Churches, Evanston, Illinois, 1954.

Dr. Kinser's eleven years as minister of the Central Christian Church, Youngstown, Ohio, was the longest pastorate in the history of that congregation. Under his leadership a beautiful new building was constructed. Erected at a cost of almost $500,000, the building was dedicated in 1950, and the remaining $200,000 debt was completely paid before Dr. Kinser's pastorate there was terminated. During this period he also served as president of the Kiwanis Club and as president of the Youngstown Ministerial Association.

Writing in the January 10, 1957, issue of "Good News," weekly organ of the Youngstown Council of Churches, the Executive Secretary, Dr. Paul W. Gauss, commented on Dr. Kinser's plans to move to Illinois:

> Strong ministers are a great blessing to the co-operative work of our Council of Churches as well as to the individual church. The Rev. Beryl Sales Kinser has been both of these in his ministry in Youngstown. We have rejoiced in his ministry in Central Christian. Here he has built a wonderful church in every sense of the word. But he has been a tower of strength in the ecumenical vision that has brought his church into a splendid fellowship with one hundred others. He leaves us soon to become pastor of one of the finest churches of his denomination. We know that we will hear fine things from the extensive ministry of Dr. Kinser.

In Springfield, Dr. Kinser continues to lead the historic First Christian Church well into the second quarter of the second century of her life and service in the kingdom of God. The congregation recently approved an extensive program of remodeling and refurbishing the beautiful building which has served for half a century.

A master in the pulpit, his sermons challenge and inspire members of a growing congregation and large numbers of visitors. He has a heart for every need, and seeks to be a teacher and mediator of the knowledge of God and of his Christ to the people of the congregation and the community. We hope that it will be many years before it becomes necessary for the church historian to add a biography of his successor.

✣ ✣ ✣

In a beautiful ceremony in the sanctuary of the historic Vine Street Christian Church in Nashville, Tennessee, on June 20, 1935, ANN BENTON ELDER became the bride of Beryl Sales Kinser, pastor of the Christian Church of Montgomery City, Missouri.

Their marriage vows were solemnized by Dr. Roger T. Nooe, the pastor at Vine Street, where Ann Elder had served as assistant organist and had studied organ with the well-known teacher and composer, May F. Lawrence. Here she had gone through all the grades of the church school, had been baptized in the hands of Dr. Cary Morgan, had shared in the life of the youth groups and had gone to young people's summer conferences. She was a graduate of Vanderbilt University with the Bachelor of Arts degree. At Vanderbilt she was a member of the Gamma Phi Beta sorority. She had also received her diploma in Art as a graduate of Ward-Belmont College. She had been privileged to receive much of her elementary education through the progressive Demonstration School of the George Peabody College for Teachers.

As the daughter of Everett Benton Elder and his wife, Ivy Johnson Elder, Ann Benton Elder was born January 16, 1912, in Chattanooga, Tennessee, where her parents were active members of the First Christian Church. The family moved to Fulton, Kentucky, for a time, and then to Nashville, Tennessee, where Mrs. Kinser's father became a watchmaker and jeweler. His hobby was firearms and he taught his young daughter, an only child, to be skillful in handling them. She has always enjoyed hunting, fishing, and camping, although her principal hobby now is in her collection of antique lamps.

Having relinquished her work as commercial artist for the Ingram Manufacturing Company, Mrs. Kinser moved with her husband to Montgomery City, Missouri. Two months later they began a new pastorate in Monroe City, Missouri. While here they welcomed David into their family. During this period, too, she continued her study of the organ with Charlotte Morris of Christian College at the same time her husband was taking special courses at the Bible College of Missouri in Columbia.

Shortly after the Kinsers moved to Clarksville, Tennessee, March 1, 1940, the organist of the Christian Church moved from the city. Mrs. Kinser was asked to supply temporarily until they could get some one as their permanent organist. The temporary assignment continued through their ministry there, interrupted briefly twice to welcome Jane, who was born December 16, 1940, and John, who was born February 12, 1945. When the Kinsers left Clarksville to go to Youngstown, Ohio, the church gave Mrs. Kinser a Hammond organ as an expression of appreciation for her ministry of music.

Mrs. Kinser is a member of the American Guild of Organists. In Youngstown she served as president of the Women's Fortnightly Club, as secretary of the Youngstown Federation of Women's Clubs, as a trustee of the Youngstown Young Women's Christian Association and as a water safety instructor with the Red Cross. These and similar interests have also been continued in Springfield and she always takes a vital, co-operative, and helpful interest in the life and work of the church.

As a wife and mother she graciously presides over her household, sharing her husband's interests and work, and following the courses which her children have chosen. David, a member of Phi Delta Theta fraternity, and a graduate in engineering science from the Case Institute of Technology in Cleveland, Ohio, is continuing as a graduate student there. Jane, a member of Delta Zeta sorority, after three years in the premedical curriculum at the University of Illinois, began her first year in the College of Medicine of the University of Illinois in Chicago in September, 1961. At the same time, John is starting in his junior year at Glenwood High School. Although the youngest member of the family, he is the first to solo fly an airplane and is awaiting his seventeenth birthday when he can qualify to take passengers cross country. For Mrs. Kinser this all comes after almost twenty years of membership in various P.T.A.'s, a stretch with the Brownies, two terms as a den mother, and a great multitude of contingencies such as every parent faces.

Dr. and Mrs. Kinser celebrated their silver wedding anniversary in 1960 on a tour of Europe where Mrs. Kinser made a special study of art and architecture, with visits to most of the great cathedrals. These are special interests which she plans to pursue with more leisure in the future.

MISSIONARIES

Susie Carson Rijnhart Moyes, M.D.

Missionary in Tibet 1903-1905

BORN: 1868, in Western Ontario

DIED: February 7, 1908, at Chatham, Ontario

MARRIED: (1) Petrus Rijnhart, 1894 (1866-1898)
Son: Charles Carson Rijnhart
Born in China June 30, 1897
Died in Tibet July 22, 1898

(2) James Moyes, 1905
Children: None

Herbert Georg Studio

Susie Carson Rijnhart Moyes

The year 1891 found Petrus Rijnhart of Rotterdam, Holland, in West China serving among the Chinese and Tibetans. Seeking funds and workers he returned to Toronto, Canada, where he had done some special studying on his way to his chosen field. Not far from Toronto he found Susie Carson, interested in foreign missions and newly graduated from medical college. They were married and in San Francisco shortly before sailing they united with the Disciples of Christ. It was in 1898 that they set forth on their long anticipated journey to Lhasa, the far interior and forbidden capital city of Tibet. Somewhere along the way their baby son died and sometime later Mr. Rijnhart disappeared. No word of his fate ever reached Dr. Rijnhart, and alone through two lonely months of perilous travel, hardship and danger she struggled back to a station of the China Inland Mission in West China where James Moyes and other missionaries looked after her and started her on her journey back to the homeland.[1]

On arriving in the United States, Dr. Rijnhart wrote a book, *With the Tibetans in Tent and Temple,* telling of her experiences and adventures. The book was widely circulated, and numerous copies are known to be in libraries and in the possession of individuals. It has been used in mission study groups and classes in all parts of the country. In this book Dr. Rijnhart tells of the plans the parents discussed for their little son as they rode along in Tibet:

> . . . We decided to give his education our personal supervision, and what books we would procure for him—the very best and most scientific in English, French and German. "He must have a happy childhood," said his father. "He shall have all the blocks, trains, rocking-horses and other things that boys in the homeland have, so that when he shall have grown up he may not feel that because he was a missionary's son, he had missed the joys that brighten other boys' lives.[2]

His bright ways had made friends for them among the natives. The baby died July 22, 1898. The drug box, emptied of its contents and lined with towels, served as a coffin. He was

---

[1]From "Biography Set, Series 5" issued by United Christian Missionary Society, 1937.

[2]"*With the Tibetans in Tent and Temple,*" by Susie Carson Rijnhart, M.D. (New York: Fleming H. Revell Company, c 1901), pp. 246-247.

buried in a grave on which was placed a large boulder to prevent desecration. Mr. Rijnhart conducted the burial service in the native tongue, so that the guide could understand,

> . . . and the cold earth of Tibet, the great forbidden land, closed over the body of the first Christian child committed to its bosom—little Charles Carson Rijnhart, aged one year, one month and twenty-two days.
>
> . . . Before leaving we covenanted that by God's help we would seek to be instrumental in sending out another missionary to Tibet, in the name of our little boy.

In his diary, dated August 23, 1898, the day of their departure, the father wrote:

> Today we started with broken hearts, leaving the body of our precious one behind in regions of eternal snow, where the mother of the Yangtse Kiang flows tranquilly past.

The disappearance of Petrus Rijnhart a few weeks later is related on page 311:

> Shouting something up to me which I did not hear on account of the rushing river, he walked up-stream in the opposite direction to the tents he had set out for. Then he followed a little path around the rocks that had obstructed our way the day before, until out of sight, and *I never saw him again.*

A government investigation resulted in a report that Petrus Rijnhart had been murdered, but that the murderer could not be traced. The report was dated "Pekin, May 2nd, 1900." No further news except vague native reports was ever received.

Dr. Rijnhart toured this country, telling her story and urging Disciples of Christ to send missionaries to Tibet. As a direct result the United Christian Missionary Society decided to open missionary work in that country.

She came to Springfield, and with the co-pastor, Hugh T. Morrison, conducted a series of rallies to awaken the missionary interest of this congregation. Starting April 27, 1902, meetings were held on successive nights in four sections of the city. The city was bisected east and west by Fifth Street, and north and south by Washington Street. This outlined four relatively equal sections or quadrants in which the church's scattered membership resided. Starting on Monday night, the first meeting of the series was held in the northwest quadrant at the home of Louis H. Coleman at First and Miller streets; on the second night in the northeast quadrant at the home of A. H. Saunders on North Sixth Street; on the third night in the southwest quadrant at the home of Judge Charles P. Kane at 1001 South Second Street; and on the fourth night in the southeast quadrant at the home of A. O. Hunsaker at 707 East Cook Street.

On Friday night, the regular prayer meeting night, a general assembly was held at the church, which proved to be a climactic spiritual experience with testimonies and prayers for divine guidance, tending to establish more firmly the congregation's will to serve in a new relation to the missionary challenge. All of the meetings were addressed by both Dr. Rijnhart and the junior pastor, Hugh T. Morrison.[3] Dr. Rijnhart returned and spoke in Springfield on November 16, 1902. The church bulletin, dated December 7, 1902, declares:

> No more advanced step has been taken by this church in recent years than that of last Sunday, when it was voted without a dissenting voice to become a Living Link church and support Dr. Susie C. Rijnhart in the foreign field. The heartiness with which the vote was given was a manifestation of the temper and ideals of our congregation.

The Foreign Christian Missionary Society appointed Dr. Rijnhart and Dr. and Mrs. A. L. Shelton as the first missionaries to Tibet. They sailed in 1903, reaching Tachienlu in 1904, and there the work was started.

In 1905 Dr. Rijnhart married James Moyes, of the China Inland Mission, a Congregationalist. In September, 1906, this

[3]Charles Clayton Morrison and Hugh T. Morrison, Jr., were copastors, 1902-1904.

church released Dr. Rijnhart in order that she might become the Living Link of the Congregationalist Church in Tacoma, Washington.

In 1907 her health became undermined by her difficult experiences and they returned to Chatham, Ontario, where she died February 7, 1908.

Rose Theresa Armbruster

Missionary in Japan 1903-1932

BORN: January 24, 1875, at Springfield, Illinois
DIED: July 14, 1950, at San Gabriel, California

Herbert Georg Studio

Rose Theresa Armbruster

Rose Theresa Armbruster was born and grew up in Springfield, Illinois. She graduated from Springfield High School in 1892. At that time the graduates took one of four different types of courses: classical course, Latin-English course, German-English course, and English or select course. She followed the German-English course.

She was employed as a grammar school teacher from 1892 to 1903. From 1893 to 1898, at the Stuart School she taught grades six and eight. She was then transferred to the Trapp School where she taught seventh grade. She also attended Hiram College. In 1903 she first went to Japan as a missionary.

Her first furlough was spent in study at the Bible Teachers' Training School in New York, and her second furlough in graduate study at Columbia University.

Miss Armbruster's particular talent was in languages. Her command of English was exceptional, and she learned Japanese in a short time, mastering the written as well as the spoken language.

Her first four years in Japan were spent in Tokyo and Osaka. She was next stationed in Akita, where she stayed until 1919. Reports of her work during these years reveal busy and enthusiastic days—making evangelistic trips through the country districts, working with the Japanese Bible women, serving a Temperance Band, and leading in Sunday School and Christian Endeavor work. A firm believer in the need of training for Sunday school teachers, she organized a city Sunday School Association in Akita and served as its president.

After another brief period in Tokyo, ill health necessitated Miss Armbruster's return to the United States in 1923. She returned to Japan in 1926 and was stationed at Osaka. There she taught in the English night school for girls and worked with the kindergarten and Mothers' Circle. When the Kizukawa Kindergarten was forced to close, the mothers' club continued to meet regularly in her home and under her guidance.

[In 1929 she became the Living Link of the Woman's Council of this church through the United Christian Missionary Society.]

Miss Armbruster returned to the United States in 1932 and retired in 1933. Until failing health prevented, she spoke frequently about Japan in the churches and carried on voluminous correspondence with her Japanese friends through which she continued to counsel and inspire them. For a time she made her home with her sister in Denver,

Colorado. She then lived at the California Christian Home, San Gabriel, California. She died July 14, 1950.[1]

The following is from "The Missionary Intelligencer," August 1917, page 385:

Biographical Sketch of Miss Rose T. Armbruster

This faithful and useful missionary comes of good, strong Teutonic blood. Not only strength, but resourcefulness and endurance are outstanding characteristics of her and of her people.

Springfield, Illinois, is the place of her birth. She was baptized in the First Christian Church in that city, November 20, 1891. During all of her experience in that congregation she was a strong, forceful, helpful member, and the church was greatly devoted to her. Her people were not members of the Christian Church. She therefore had some problems to solve in taking the step her mind and heart prompted her to take in accepting the position and fellowship of the Disciples of Christ. The teaching of our people made a strong appeal to her independent mind. The congregation at Springfield took pride in the fine character and in the all-round useful life of this new member. Miss Armbruster soon became a real factor in the social life of the congregation.

. . . Her pride in exactness, her constant hunger for knowledge, her delight in a wide range of information, her tenacity in the prosecution of her studies, soon ranked her among the best students and the ripest scholars of that city of high standards in literary attainments. Springfield is no mean city.

. . . Japan made a strong appeal to her vivid imagination, her strong sentiment, and to her best judgment. . . . Japan was rising before the world in power and leadership. She saw clearly that the "Sunrise Kingdom" was to become one of the most dominant influences in the Far East. Her wide range of information about Japan and her good judgment helped her to accurately interpret the situation. . . . The decision to go to Japan was a wise one.

. . . She arrived in Japan October 17, 1903, as a missionary of the Foreign Society. . . . She was an influence of force wherever she went. Her presence encouraged the missionaries and won the confidence and admiration of the Japanese.

---

[1]From *They Went to Japan,* United Christian Missionary Society, 1949, page 23.

Dr. Arthur Paul Wakefield

Medical Missionary in China 1904-1927

BORN: October 5, 1878, at Bloomfield, Ohio
DIED: February 6, 1942, at Boston, Massachusetts
MARRIED: Olive Catharine Lindsay, June 14, 1904
CHILDREN: Vachel Lindsay Wakefield, born April 17, 1906, in Wuhu, China

Mary Churchill Wakefield, born May 18, 1908, in Springfield, Illinois; died March 8, 1916, in China

Catharine Frazee Wakefield, born September 26, 1913, in Wuhu, China

Martha Isabelle Wakefield, born May 4, 1915, in Wuhu, China

Herbert Georg Studio

Arthur Paul Wakefield

Herbert Georg Studio

Olive Catharine Lindsay Wakefield

In the Illinois State Historical Library is a book of genealogy entitled *Ancestral Lines of the Doniphan, Frazee and Hamilton Families,* by Frances Frazee Hamilton, which incidentally traces the lineage of Olive Catharine Lindsay Wakefield. The section devoted to Arthur Paul Wakefield includes his account of his own lineage, together with many important facts in his adventurous and distinguished career.

Dr. Arthur Paul Wakefield . . . is a direct descendant of Governor William Bradford, governor for thirty-five years of the Plymouth Colony, 1621-1657. Governor Bradford was born in Austerfield Yorkshire, England, March, 1590.

Dr. Wakefield is the son of Professor Edmund Burritt Wakefield and his wife, Martha Sheldon Wakefield. Professor Wakefield moved with his family when Paul was nine years of age from Bloomfield, Ohio, to Hiram, where Paul graduated in 1900 with the degree of Ph.B. In 1904, Dr. Wakefield received the degree of M.D. at Rush Medical College, University of Chicago. In 1906, he received the degree of A.M. from Bethany College, West Virginia. On June 14, 1904, he married Olive Catharine Lindsay of Springfield, Illinois, daughter of Dr. and Mrs. Vachel Thomas Lindsay, and sister of America's illustrious poet, Vachel Lindsay.

In 1905 Dr. Wakefield was sent by the Foreign Board of the Christian Church as a medical missionary to China. He and his wife landed at Shanghai on Thanksgiving Day, 1905. They were stationed at Nanking, Chuchow, Wuhu and Luchowfu until 1918. While in Wuhu, Dr. Wakefield spent almost a year in sanitation work, in connection with the rebuilding of the Yangtsze River dyke. This work required a force of seven thousand men. Dr. Wakefield's work was so efficient that this task was completed without the appearance of the famine fever so prevalent in China. [For this he was decorated by the Chinese National Red Cross.]

At Luchowfu, Dr. Wakefield did hospital work. This town was the home of China's great statesman, Li Hung Chang, who was a personal friend of Dr. Wakefield, employing Dr. Wakefield as his family physician. While in Luchowfu, Dr. Wakefield gave nearly thirty-five thousand medical treatments. While at Luchowfu, he accepted a call from the Episcopalian Board as Instructor of Student Health at Boone University at Wuchang.

[In 1920 the Wakefields were confirmed in Wuchang as members of the Episcopal Church, and served thereafter under the Board of the Protestant Episcopal Church. Dr. Wakefield was officially appointed by the Episcopal Board May 11, 1920, as missionary to Hankow, China.]

At Boone University, Wuchang, Dr. Wakefield was head of the student health. His was the first real student health work done in China. Under Dr. Wakefield, the Chinese youths developed physically as they advanced in school until the graduates passed a grade-A life insurance examination. When these young men entered Boone, they were no less than twenty-five per cent tubercular. He was stationed at Wuchang during the entire siege of the late war, administering medical aid to the opposing generals and their armies. He was one of the besieged of Wuchang when that city was confined within closed gates for twenty-nine days, having on hand but one week's supply of rations. Prior to this, Dr. Wakefield had sent his wife and two daughters to Japan for safety; the son, Vachel, was already in the United States, a student of Hiram College. Before the siege of Wuchang ended there was suffering, starvation and death on every hand; Dr. Wakefield suffering with the others. It was through his solicitation that the city gates were opened. In his judgment all would perish if they remained inside, but some might escape if the gates were opened. During this siege, Dr. Wakefield, through his profession, was a friend of both generals and it was through his influence the siege finally ended. In the *Chicago Daily Tribune* for October 9, 1926, appeared the following with glaring headlines, which referred to Dr. Wakefield:

YANKEE'S DARING WINS PEACE FOR BESIEGED CITY

Doctor's Courage Brings Cantonese to Terms

Wuchang, China, October 8 [1926]—The chairman of the Chamber of Commerce and the Chinese Red Cross assure *The Tribune* that the American Episcopalians were solely responsible for the evacuation of the starving inhabitants in the city of Wuchang, besieged for thirty-nine days, and for the initiation of the surrender to the Cantonese. Dr. Wakefield of the Episcopal hospital staff was particularly responsible, having won the Cantonese general's confidence when the latter thought he was dying from a heavy draft of poison.

The bottle was not labeled, but Dr. Wakefield sniffed of it, and believed it was lime juice. He drank the contents before the general, and then applied an emetic. This enabled the Americans to become mediators.

DR. WAKEFIELD'S OWN ACCOUNT OF HIS FAMILY LINEAGE

The Commonwealth of Massachusetts
Department of Public Health
State House, Boston

October 14, 1928

My family history I know little about, but have it all in a "Book" in China. In general, Wakefields came very early to New England. The first grave in the first burying ground in Boston is a Wakefield—direct line. I am 10th generation, so am pretty near pure "U. S." My family (Wakefields) moved to Ohio in 1812. Settled in Western Reserve (Trumbull County). Grandmother (Churchill) Wakefield's mother was a Bradford; her Uncle William Bradford came to her home, lived and died with her. Hopelessly crusty, unmarried, he was devoted to Grandmother. These two were in direct line from Governor Bradford.

All his life [grandfather's] he farmed, bought and sold cattle, preached, married, buried people, always with no pay. He was a founder of Hiram College.

Father went to Hiram, one year to Bethany to meet the Campbell-Bethany groups; studied science. He was on the original Yellowstone survey, from there went to Tucson, Arizona, interested in mining; lost everything just before I was born (1878). He had preached at Tucson on a dare. He felt that when the Lord's Day came there should be religious services. In the face of the dare he preached unmolested. When he came home a church at North Bloomfield (five miles from Grandfather) needed a pastor, so father served that church. I was born while he lived at Bloomfield. He never got away from the pulpit after that. Hiram called him after a pastorate of seven years in Warren, Ohio, about 1882-1889, and all the rest of his life he lived in Hiram.

He had a genius for teaching. In father's classes any boy of average brain power could get his stuff over at the end of the term by listening in during class. So he had a reputation of being easy. One could not attend his classes and not learn; and now old students who did not appreciate him then remember his teaching. He has in Hiram now the standing as a teacher that he should have had twenty and more years ago and still his standing keeps on growing. Three times he filled in as Acting President. He refused the office itself; he hated executive work and was not fitted for it. But faculty and students backed him loyally when he had to fill in. He is the greatest (truly great) man I have ever known and I have a very unholy pride in being his son. I never heard him speak unkindly to or of any one. He never "rode" a student, and a student in trouble had father always as his friend. Many a boy owes his salvation to my father's patience, tolerance and deep affection. The greatest sorrows he ever knew were when boys occasionally betrayed his trust. Even then his pain was for the future of such a fellow. What could he do to save him? To bring his best out! Father always meant that when he so often said, "We must bring that boy out."

Mother was also pioneer stock, she was a Sheldon. Her Grandfather Gersham came from Connecticut in 1800 to survey the northeast corner of Western Reserve for Connecticut. He came horseback with his bride, making the trip in 57 days. He had the next survey section to Cleveland. This enters in Portage County, and here on the old Indian portage from Lake (via Cuyahoga River) to Gulf down the Mahoning and Ohio Rivers, he built his colonial home. Grandmother was a Daw, a wonderfully efficient and determined woman. Mother met father in Hiram. Father, bashful, diffident to the last day of life, fell madly in love with "Mathie" (Martha) Sheldon, the most beautiful girl in school. She had sense to understand and appreciate father, took him and stuck to him. She stood by him through life. Our home was open house to everyone all my life. Mother did practically all the work. We never made a fuss over anyone who came, but high, low, rich, poor came. Father and mother gave everything to their friends, and everyone was friend, especially those who had any need, physical, spiritual or mental. How they lived on the salary father got I do not know. But I do know this—they are the richest people I have ever known.

For myself. Sick from nine to sixteen years I grew up a semi-invalid, no athletics, only playing with girls. Then I went into gymnasium and fought it out, breaking up adhesion of the old appendix.

We came home on furlough in 1917. Under the Rockefeller Fellowship I studied in Harvard Tropical School, Resident M.D. in South Department Boston City Hospital, and in Westfield State Tubercular Sanitorium for Children. Returned to China and in 1919 I went to Boone University, Wuchang, as head of Student Health, where we remained until returning to the United States December, 1927.

I went through the siege of Wuchang; and with B. P. Gilman acted as messenger in carrying papers for surrender of the city. After the entry of the Canton-Russian force we had to work to save our property. After the Nanking affair I was left virtually alone with the Chinese (faculty) staff; finally we had to smuggle our leading Chinese on to British boats to save them and close the school (May 1927). I was made Acting Dean and got authority from the Trustees to graduate our Seniors, which I did in Hankow Cathedral, it being impossible to have a graduation in our school buildings in Wuchang. I spent the summer in Japan, resting, and, no possibility of my work reopening, I finally left Hankow for home via Suez in October, 1927.

I was offered, by cable, the position of Supervisor of State Tuberculosis Clinics (Massachusetts). I got into New York December 20th, 1927, and began this work January 1st, 1928.

For record I did post-graduate work at Hiram for A. M., did not do my thesis. I wanted to clear this, as A.M. counts in China. I wrote home to Father about it. He read the letter to Thomas Phillips, who was Trustee of Bethany. Phillips said nothing to father but went to Bethany and had them give me an A.M. This was such a pretty tribute to Father that I have let it go and have never taken my Hiram A.M., but do accept, with no little feeling of pride and humility, the Bethany Degree.

While on his way home in 1927, Dr. Wakefield was offered, by cable, the position of supervisor of Tuberculosis Clinics in the Division of Sanatoria and Tuberculosis Control, Department of Public Health of the Commonwealth of Massachusetts, and began the work on January 1, 1928. His office was in the statehouse at Boston. He remained there until October 31, 1932, when he accepted a position in Central Maine Sanatorium, at Fairfield, Maine. On July 31, 1936, he returned to the Department of Public Health of Massachusetts, working with the Services for Crippled Children, and stayed with that work until his death. Upon the death of Dr. Wakefield, the Department of Public Health of Massachusetts adopted the following resolutions:

ARTHUR PAUL WAKEFIELD, M.D.

WHEREAS, Dr. Arthur Paul Wakefield of Belmont, Massachusetts, Supervisor of Clinics for Crippled Children in the Massachusetts Department of Public Health, died February 6, 1942; and

WHEREAS, Dr. Wakefield's entire professional life both in this country and abroad was devoted to the service of his fellow men in the varied roles of physician, teacher and leader; and

WHEREAS, his services in Massachusetts contributed materially toward familiarizing the people of the Commonwealth with the work of this department; and

WHEREAS, Dr. Wakefield in his private as well as his professional life displayed a sincerity, a singleness of purpose, and a kindliness that endeared him to his friends and associates, to whom his passing comes as a personal loss; be it therefore

RESOLVED, That the Department of Public Health of Massachusetts hereby formally recognize, with sincere appreciation, the services of Dr. Arthur Paul Wakefield to the Commonwealth and his loss to the cause of public health.

That it express its regret at his death and extend its deep sympathy to his widow and children, and that a copy of this resolution of esteem and sympathy be spread upon the records of the Department and that a copy be transmitted to his widow and children.

A biographical sketch of Dr. Wakefield appears in *Who's Who in America* in 7 biennial issues, from Volume 17, 1932-1933, page 2359, to and including Volume 23, 1944-1945, page 2204.

✣ ✣ ✣

MRS. OLIVE CATHARINE LINDSAY WAKEFIELD was born October 10, 1877, at Springfield, Illinois. She was the older sister of Nicholas Vachel Lindsay, the poet. Her parents were Dr. Vachel T. Lindsay and Esther Catharine Frazee Lindsay.

She and her brother, Vachel, graduated from Springfield High School in 1897. Both attended Hiram College, where she received the degree of A.B. in 1901. She next attended the Boston School of Oratory for one year. She taught English in Springfield High School in 1902-1903. On June 14, 1904, she married Arthur Paul Wakefield, newly graduated as a medical doctor from Rush Medical College, and went with him, in 1905, to China as medical missionaries, sent by the Foreign Christian Missionary Society of the Disciples of Christ. In *World Call,* March 1919, page 61, mention is made of Mrs. Wakefield teaching at Luchowfu, China.

Dr. and Mrs. Arthur Paul Wakefield have the distinction of serving as missionaries under two Protestant denominations —Disciples of Christ and Protestant Episcopal Church. They served under Disciples of Christ until 1920. At that time, as related by Mrs. Wakefield, her husband decided to go into the field of preventive medicine, and applied for appointment on the staff at Boone University at Wuchang, China, which was owned and operated by the Protestant Episcopal Church. He was accepted with the provision that Dr. and Mrs. Wakefield should take membership in that denomination. In 1920 they were confirmed in Wuchang, thus becoming members of the Episcopal church.

A daughter, Catharine Wakefield (Mrs. Paul Ward), in a letter of March 15, 1961, says:

> I remember hearing my father say that he felt that he was now fully a member of both churches—that it was a wider communion rather than a substitution of one for the other. I know that my mother, too, regarded the First Christian Church in Springfield as the center of her church life—to which other memberships might from time to time be added.

After their return to this country in 1927, Mrs. Wakefield placed her membership in Christ Episcopal Church at Cambridge, Massachusetts, and took up activity for that parish in work with foreign students in the metropolitan Boston area. After Dr. Wakefield's death, Olive Lindsay Wakefield transferred her membership from that church to Christ Episcopal Church in Springfield, Illinois, on August 31, 1945. The parish record there shows that on June 21, 1946, she "defected to the First Christian Church, Springfield, Illinois, the church of her birth." She lived in the old Lindsay home until her death. She wrote extensively and lectured on the life and work of her brother, Vachel Lindsay, the poet. She organized prayer circles of young people who met at her house. Not long before her death she sold the Lindsay house to the Vachel Lindsay House Fund, Inc., which has restored the building and made it a shrine, visited regularly by thousands of persons. She was a regular attendant at this church while health permitted.

She died May 2, 1957.

Mrs. Mary Luranah Randall Hall

Missionary in India 1947-1953

BORN: May 15, 1916, in Central Illinois
MARRIED: William David Hall (born October 25, 1914), June 26, 1938
CHILDREN: David Randall Hall, born in Tennessee
Bruce Fletcher Hall, born in India
Sarah Wynne Hall, born in India

Herbert Georg Studio

Mary Luranah Randall Hall

Mrs. William David Hall became this church's missionary link in India in 1947. Her career, as a missionary and since, is so interwoven with that of her husband that we quote from page 155 of *They Went to India,* published by the United Christian Missionary Society in 1954:

Twice Mr. and Mrs. William David Hall have had a share in the beginnings of very promising projects, the fulfillment of which they were not to see. This happened first in Livingston, Tennessee, where the Dale Hollow Larger Parish was little more than a dream when the Halls sailed for India; and on their first furlough physical disability prevented their returning to India to help in the development of the new work in Orissa.

The Halls both come of middle-western farm people. Mrs. Hall was Mary Lu Randall, and she grew up on a farm in Illinois where she early learned the meaning of hard work. Bill also grew up on an Illinois farm, and his family expected him to follow the tradition of three generations of Halls at Hall Hill Farm [near Mechanicsburg].

Mary Lu worked to pay most of her expenses during high school and college. Bill had always found time for music, athletics, and other extracurricular activities. After he met Mary Lu, through the student work at University Place Church while they were both students at the University of Illinois, his "extra-curriculars" centered around her.

After the university years, Bill taught for two years, and then enrolled in Yale Divinity School. Mary Lu, having graduated with honors, worked at the University for a year. Then, in 1938, the college romance culminated in their marriage, and they shared three busy years at Yale. Bill, in addition to studying at the university, was minister of education at the Congregational Church of Danbury, Connecticut.

In 1941, the Halls were accepted for service in India, Bill graduated from Yale, was ordained, and they both enrolled at Cornell for a special course in agriculture and home economics for rural missionaries.

War conditions made it impossible to go to India in 1942 and the Halls began home mission work at Livingston Academy, Livingston, Tennessee. They remained there until July, 1945.

Mr. Hall was accepted by the rural mountain people in a fine way. Under his influence, the missionary spirit in the Livingston church came alive, and the church began a systematic financial program. His leadership of group singing was a real contribution, and he was in demand for our own and interdenominational young people's conferences and retreats over a wide area. He developed an interdenominational youth program with Methodist and Christian churches which resulted in the establishment of a youth center after he left. Out of a joint enterprise with the Alpine Presbyterian Mission grew the beginnings of the Dale Hollow Larger Parish, which is now serving the area effectively.

Mrs. Hall occasionally substituted both in her husband's Bible classes and in some of the high school science classes. She helped to produce the church paper and was active in the life of the church, the school, and the community. She kept their home a pleasant and inviting place for the many who came to see them, and often entertained the young people and other groups from the church.

The Halls landed in Calcutta on January 9, 1946. They were stationed in Takhatpur for part-time work, which easily became full-time as soon as the language exams were behind them. Takhatpur is a rural district, and the Halls travelled over a vast and roadless area, maintaining the fellowship and guidance for the scattered village congregations.

In the fall of 1948 they were temporarily assigned to the Allahabad Agricultural Institute, an interdenominational agricultural college. Mr. Hall served as acting head of the Extension Department.

In 1949 they took up residence in Bilaspur to oversee the evangelistic work and village churches of the area. Here Mr. Hall developed an audio-visual village evangelistic program, coordinating in a total program the use of movies, film strips and slides, flannelgraph, public address system, and recordings. This combination of methods proved highly successful in drawing crowds.

Mr. Hall had several hobbies which contributed to the effectiveness of his missionary service. A "shutter-bug," he sent dozens of pictures to America every year, many of which have appeared in *World Call* and other publications.

An interest in youth work developed in two directions. He edited a recreational manual which has been used all over India and is being edited for a second edition. He wrote a youth manual for local churches. This was published in Hindi, is being used all over the Hindi-speaking area, and has been translated for use in some areas of South India. Also he took an active part in young people's conferences, served for two years as convener of the youth work committee of the Mid-India Representative Christian Council which involved ex-officio membership on the N. C. C. youth work committee. This interest also caused his vacations to be a busman's holidays, because he gave much of his vacation time to recreational leadership for, and informal counseling with, the young people at Woodstock School.

Because of Mr. Hall's interest and ability in the audio-visual program, the Halls were among the first of our missionaries to explore the new field of co-operation with the British Baptists in Orissa. They brought an enthusiastic recommendation to the annual mission convention, and en route to America were able to attend meetings of the Baptist Missionary Society in England.

The lifting and carrying of heavy audio-visual equipment while Mr. Hall was in India aggravated an old injury and caused the disability which prevented their return to the field.

In 1953 the Halls came back to this country on furlough. Mrs. Hall spoke from our pulpit at the Sunday morning service. Mr. Hall showed scores of slides at an evening dinner meeting, illustrating their work in India.

In 1953 Mr. Hall became a member of the staff of the United Christian Missionary Society and moved to Indianapolis. The problem of setting up housekeeping again in this country after an absence of several years was such that Mary Lu says she considered writing a book on "How to get along without what you have to have." In August, 1956, Mr. Hall became a member of the faculty at Brite Bible College of Texas Christian University, and the family moved to Fort Worth, Texas, where they now live. Both work in the International Student Committee. Texas Christian University has over 50 students from abroad, who often need help when they arrive on a strange campus in a strange country. Mr. Hall is sponsor of the Student Volunteer Movement, among other activities. Mary Lu thus describes herself (October 18, 1960):

Still and all, I consider myself a homemaker, and I take on only those outside activities which I can work into my schedule without being away from home when the children come from school. I do my own housework and like to have time to make clothes for Sarah and myself, and to work in the yard. I like the climate and Texas and Texans, and we all seem to have put down roots, and are very happy living here.

Her present address is 2825 Merida, Fort Worth, Texas.

Mrs. Elizabeth Anne Eastman Mills

Missionary in Paraguay, 1954-

BORN: March 29, 1900, at Minneapolis, Minnesota
MARRIED: John Raymond Mills, August 20, 1930
CHILDREN: John Eastman Mills
Elizabeth Lee Mills (Young)

Herbert Georg Studio

Elizabeth Anne Eastman Mills

Part of the story of Elizabeth (Betty) Mills and her husband, John Raymond Mills, is told in *They Went to Latin America,* published in 1947 by the United Christian Missionary Society:

> John Raymond and Elizabeth Anne Eastman Mills had a varied Christian experience over a wide field of service before they went to Paraguay in 1937.
>
> John Raymond was born in Indiana, but was taken by his parents at an early age to California. He did his elementary and high school work in Alhambra, California, schools; received his B.A. degree from Pomona College, his M.A. from the Hartford School of Religion, and his B.D. from the Hartford Theological Seminary. He also did special work in the College of Missions and in Columbia University. He earned about half of his way through school doing construction work, waiting on tables, as salesman, and in Y.M.C.A. and church work. He was baptized in 1916 by the Reverend J. Walter Carpenter. He is a product of a missionary-minded Christian home, and from an early age was active in Christian service. To his parents he gives the honor of being those who most influenced him to dedicate his life to missionary work. After them, he mentions Dr. A. L. Shelton and the young people's conference movement.
>
> Elizabeth Eastman was born in Minneapolis, Minnesota, and did her elementary and high school work in her home city. She took her B.A. and B.S. degrees from the University of Minnesota, and did special work in the Kennedy School of Missions. She was baptized in Springfield, Massachusetts, by the great missionary statesman, Andrew F. Hensey.

Of the influences which brought her to the decision to give her life to missionary work she says: "I was brought up in a Christian home where everyone was keenly interested in missions."

Upon the graduation of John Raymond Mills from Pomona College in California in 1927, his father offered to take him into his real estate and insurance business. However, Raymond had a deep desire to enter Christian work. While deciding what to do, an opportunity came to take a summer course at Columbia University and then go to a mission school in Izmir,

Turkey, to teach for three years and to serve as treasurer of the institution. His father and mother were tithers and had always worked faithfully in the church. Their deep concern for the church and missions took root in Raymond.

While in Turkey, he met a young lady by the name of Elizabeth Anne Eastman whom he asked to become his bride. Upon returning to the United States in 1930, they were married in Minneapolis, Minnesota. They were convinced that they wanted to enter foreign missionary service, so they entered Hartford Theological Seminary where Raymond secured his divinity degree and his Master of Arts degree. He was kept busy serving in churches while his wife, Betty, worked as a social case worker in Hartford, Connecticut, in order to solve financial problems. The United Christian Missionary Society also helped with grants in order that they might prepare for missionary work in China. During the depression years missionaries were being brought home, so the Board could not send them out.

In 1934 Dr. Raphael H. Miller had gone to the National City Christian Church at Washington, D. C. as pastor and he needed an associate. Raymond and Betty were called to assist in the work at the National City Church where they stayed for over three years. Both were ordained to the ministry there.

In 1937 a missionary family needed to be replaced in our International College in Asuncion, Paraguay. Raymond and Betty were asked by the United Christian Missionary Society to go to Paraguay as missionaries. They taught together in the school for fifteen years, when there came to them a dream to open a church and settlement house among the poor of the city. In October, 1953, Friendship Mission was inaugurated and their dream became a reality with the help of the school alumni, churches, and friends.

Friendship Mission is meeting a need presented by Communism, poverty, and illiteracy. The Colegio Internacional (International College) at Asuncion, capital of Paraguay, educates the children of the well-to-do. Friendship Mission works among the lower classes. The mission represents a co-operative effort between the alumni of Colegio Internacional and the United Christian Missionary Society. Through the efforts of the alumni the Paraguayan government sold the land to the Society at a reduced price as a gesture of good will. The alumni contributed materials, services, and money. The North American committee and friends gave generously. The mission has thirteen buildings constructed on over a city block of land. It has a large playground, a small football field, and three basketball courts where children and young people play under supervision.

Among the activities are: bathhouses for boys and for girls, eagerly patronized; a dental clinic, 6 mornings each week; a medical clinic, 2 mornings each week; a kindergarten, 5 mornings each week; typing classes, 2 a day; sewing classes, 4 a day; English classes, 2 a day.

All services are free.

Mr. and Mrs. Mills have two children who are married and live in Southern California—John E. Mills and Elizabeth L. Mills (Young).

Mrs. Elizabeth Anne Eastman Mills became the mission link of First Christian Church in 1953, succeeding Mary Lu Hall, 1947-1953. In 1953 the United Christian Missionary Society decided not to return William David Hall and his wife Mary Lu to the mission field in India, but made Mr. Hall a member of its staff. The First Christian Church thereupon applied to the U. C. M. S. for permission to make Mrs. Elizabeth Anne Eastman Mills its missionary link. She and Mr. Mills had recently opened Friendship Mission in Asuncion, Paraguay. Both Mr. and Mrs. Mills came to the United States on furlough in 1955, in the course of which they visited this church for several days, telling of their work. In particular they emphasized the need of a new station wagon to take the place of one that was rapidly losing its usefulness. The World Work Department of this church planned a campaign to raise $3,000 for the purpose and succeeded in raising $3,105, which was turned over to Mr. and Mrs. Mills. They purchased the station wagon and used it in this country for about a month before shipping it to Asuncion. The total cost including customs duty was about $4,000. In a letter of thanks, Mrs. Mills said:

> The old car which is over seven years old, and will be replaced by this new one, has been used for every possible service imaginable. You can well imagine the many uses of such a car at Friendship Mission. It will serve for hauling supplies of all kinds and to transport doctors, dentists, and other people serving the Mission. It will be used as an ambulance to carry the sick to and from hospitals; to carry members of our church to special meetings in other parts of the city; to transport eqiupment and people to our conference grounds thirty miles out into the country. And what a help it will be in evangelistic calling and in our alumni work, for distances are great.

In addition, the Chi Rho Society of this church engaged in a campaign selling sacks of sand, resulting in a gift of $500 toward the completion of an addition to one of the buildings at Friendship Mission. Also the church contributed $500 toward the building of a swimming pool at a conference ground near Asuncion, and other gifts. Several young people in the church have been corresponding with young people at Friendship Mission. Mrs. Mills acts as interpreter if necessary.

Mr. and Mrs. Mills send a monthly letter to the church, reporting on their doings. The World Work Department circulates the letter and sends it to a mailing list of over fifty members of the church. This keeps the membership fairly well informed, and stimulates a continuing interest in what is done and what needs to be done.

The labors of Mr. and Mrs. Mills cover a large portion of the missionary work of the Christian Church (Disciples of Christ) in South America, notably in the country of Paraguay and in Brazil and Argentina. Mr. Mills is treasurer of the U. C. M. S. for the entire country of Paraguay. All money for the missions passes through his hands. At Asuncion, for many years, Mr. Mills has been President of the "Patronata de Leprosas del Paraguay," a national association including many Paraguayans of prominence, to carry on the fight against Hansen's disease (leprosy).

Mr. and Mrs. Mills again visited this church for several days during their furlough in 1960. Mrs. Mills preached at the Sunday morning church service, while Mr. Mills talked to the combined adult classes at church school on religious conditions in Paraguay. They were in constant demand for conferences with numerous groups.

Two members of this congregation visited Friendship Mission in 1956. Miss Lucy Williams traveled with a group of 30 in May, visiting missions of the Disciples of Christ in South America, culminating at Buenos Aires in the celebration of the fiftieth anniversary of the establishment of the mission in that area. Their tour included a day at Friendship Mission. Later, in July, Charles Foster McElroy spent a week as the guest of Mr. and Mrs. Mills and had a chance to see practically all of the activities of Friendship Mission. He also visited the mission at Coronel Oviedo in Paraguay. Both Miss Williams and Mr. McElroy have only the highest praise for what they saw in Paraguay.

Herbert Georg Studio

Portraits of Ministers
of the
First Christian Church
Springfield, Illinois
Given in Memory of
Cora Clarke McElroy
by her Husband
Charles Foster McElroy
September 21, 1958

Ministers Whose Portraits
Were Not Available:

Josephus Hewitt, 1833-1835
Jeremiah P. Lancaster, 1841-1843
William M. Brown, 1843-1847
Alexander Johnson, 1852-1854
B. F. Perky, 1854-1856
James B. Crane, 1871-1872
Joseph Buford Allen, 1879-1883
John Z. Taylor, 1883-1884

Herbert Georg Stud

IN MEMORIAM

The portraits shown here, uniformly framed, hang in two rows on the wall of a long corridor between the sanctuary and the education building of First Christian Church of Springfield, Illinois. They include 24 pastors, 21 wives, and 6 missionaries—51 in all. Among them is a "presentation" frame reciting that they constitute a memorial to Cora Clarke McElroy, given by her husband, Charles Foster McElroy. Smaller photographs of Mr. and Mrs. McElroy are included in the frame, with a list of the eight pastors whose likenesses were not available:

No. 1 Josephus Hewitt, pastor, 1833-1835
No. 3 Jeremiah P. Lancaster, pastor, 1841-1843
No. 4 William M. Brown, pastor, 1843-1847
No. 7 Alexander Johnson, pastor, 1852-1854
No. 8 B. F. Perky, pastor, 1854-1856
No. 13 James B. Crane, pastor, 1871-1872
No. 17 Joseph Buford Allen, pastor, 1879-1883
No. 18 John Z. Taylor, pastor, 1883-1884

The portraits were presented to the church at the morning worship service on September 21, 1958, by Mr. McElroy, who said:

On the "Fountain of Time" in Washington Park, Chicago, is inscribed:

"Time goes, they say. Ah no!
Time stays; we go."

Herbert Georg Studio

TOP ROW: Alexander Graham—Andrew J. Kane, Mrs. Kane—John H. Hughes—Sterling E. Pearre, Mrs. Pearre—Daniel R. Howe—Lanceford B. Wilkes, Mrs. Wilkes—Thomas T. Holton, Mrs. Holton—Harvey W. Everest, Mrs. Everest—Edward T. Williams, Mrs. Williams—John M. Atwater, Mrs. Atwater—Ely V. Zollars, Mrs. Zollars—John B. Briney, Mrs. Briney—Abner P. Cobb, Mrs. Cobb—Jay Elwood Lynn, Mrs. Lynn.

Herbert Georg Studio

BOTTOM ROW: Hugh T. Morrison, Mrs. H. T. Morrison—Charles Clayton Morrison, Mrs. C. C. Morrison—Frederick W. Burnham, Mrs. Burnham—Frank Waller Allen, Mrs. Allen—William F. Rothenburger, Mrs. Rothenburger—Clark W. Cummings, Mrs. Cummings—Charles B. Tupper, Mrs. Tupper—Harry M. Davis, Mrs. Davis—James N. Gibble, Mrs. Gibble—Beryl Sales Kinser, Mrs. Kinser (Presentation—In Memoriam). *(Missionaries):* Mrs. Susie C. Rijnhart-Moyes—Rose Theresa Armbruster—Dr. Arthur Paul Wakefield, Mrs. (Olive Lindsay) Wakefield—Mary Lu (Mrs. William D.) Hall—Elizabeth (Mrs. J. Raymond) Mills.

The history of a church is primarily its record as a congregation, as evidenced in our recent observance of the 125th anniversary of First Christian Church of Springfield, Illinois. But in a large measure that record is shaped by those who have served as pastors, with their spiritual insight, constructive ideas, and practical methods. During this church's 125 years it has had 32 ministers. We believe it is proper that we should give recognition to their leadership by preserving for ourselves and posterity their likenesses in portrait form. It is equally fitting that their wives should be honored. The wife of a pastor shares his labors and takes a place of leadership in the routine functioning of the church. Also, the missionaries who have gone out from this church, or who have acted as our missionary links on foreign fields, merit this type of appreciation.

Of the 32 ministers we have been able to procure portraits of 24; we have 15 portraits of wives, and 5 of missionaries—making 44 in all. We hope to be able to obtain still others.

Procuring these portraits has occupied four years. In particular I wish to thank Dr. Harry M. Davis, our pastor in 1954, for helping to initiate and carry on our quest for them. And I wish to thank the photographer, Herbert Georg, for his personal interest and attention in giving to these the highest photographic excellence.

My wife was a member of this church and she was sensitive to the beauty of our building. We trust that this type of memorial is in keeping with the innate loveliness of this structure. My son, George Clarke McElroy, is present with his wife, and they join me in presenting to First Christian Church these portraits in memory of his mother, Cora Clarke McElroy.

The portraits were accepted by H. L. Allison, chairman of the General Board. At that time the number of portraits was 44. Since then likenesses of 6 wives and 1 missionary have been added, making a present total of 51.

We hope for more. Can any of our readers help in locating others?

CORA CLEONA CLARKE McELROY

Cora Cleona Clarke was born December 4, 1881, on a farm near Edinburg, Indiana. She graduated from Franklin College in 1905, and taught for several years in high schools at Newport, Brazil and Franklin in Indiana, and Kalispell in Montana. On August 4, 1913, she was married to Charles Foster McElroy and lived in or near Chicago until 1943, when they moved to Springfield, Illinois, and united with the First Christian Church. They had one son, George Clarke McElroy. She was an authority on bird life, and contributed regularly to the Audubon publications. She was a member of Pen Women of America. She died November 23, 1950.

Date Due

JUN 25 '71			